Bible Study Guide and Workbook for Beginners

How to Easily Understand Every Book of the Bible—With Clear Lessons and Practical Exercises

Welcome Aboard, Check Out This Limited-Time Free Bonus!

Ahoy, reader! Welcome to the Ahoy Publications family, and thanks for snagging a copy of this book! Since you've chosen to join us on this journey, we'd like to offer you something special.

Check out the link below for a FREE e-book filled with delightful facts about American History.

But that's not all - you'll also have access to our exclusive email list with even more free e-books and insider knowledge. Well, what are ye waiting for? Click the link below to join and set sail toward exciting adventures in American History.

Access your bonus here
https://ahoypublications.com/
Or, Scan the QR code!

Table of Contents

Part 1: Bible Study for Beginners

Unlocking the Essentials with Beginner-Friendly and Easy-to-Understand Explanations

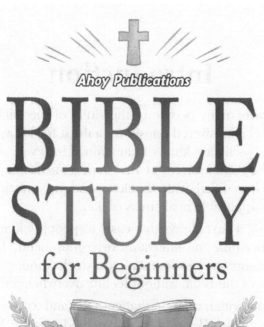

Introduction

What often attracts many people to the study of the Bible is a quest for answers to several unanswered questions, a thirst for knowledge, or simply a stumble-upon-by-chance kind of situation. However, regardless of the initial reason, they often arrive at the same conclusion: The Bible is a treasure trove. It is filled with timeless wisdom, practical lessons, and insightful stories applicable in all areas of life.

Simply reading it isn't always that easy, as people often give up as they find it too cumbersome to understand or comprehend. *Where to begin?* Seems to be a common question. Are you stuck wondering where to start your exploration of the Bible without feeling overwhelmed?

This book was written to erase that concern and to give you easy access to the treasures of the Bible. The Bible Study Guide for Beginners is more than just a book; it's a guide that holds your hand and helps you navigate the timeless stories and teachings within the pages of the Bible. It guides you through the revelations of many of the most important chapters – Genesis, Exodus, Psalms, Proverbs, Matthew, Romans, Hebrews, down to Revelation. This exploration is a marathon, not a sprint, so you are encouraged to enjoy each passage at your own pace. As much of an insightful read as the Bible is, this guide will make it just as enjoyable. See it as having a casual chat about the scriptures.

So, if you've always wanted to explore the Bible but felt unsure about where to begin, consider this book your friendly companion and guide. It promises to make your journey of the Bible less complicated and more enjoyable. A life-changing discovery awaits you on the other side!

Note: There are several versions of the Bible written at different times – but mainly with the aim of improving readability – NOT changing its content or meaning. This book will use different versions, including the King James Version, the NIV (New International Version), and the NKJV (the New King James Version).

Chapter 1: Genesis Unveiled

It has been said that there is no fixed way to go about the study of the Bible or in what order it should be read. This is indeed true, but a good suggestion would be to start from where it all began. *Genesis* is the first book of the Bible, which literally means "beginning." It is also in line with the Hebrew title, which was coined from the first three words in Genesis, "in the beginning," which is translated into Biblical Hebrew as *Bereshit*. In the pages of Genesis lies the beauty of the unique formation and creation of the world.

Genesis is the first book of the Bible.[1]

The Book of Genesis is one part of a five-book volume referred to as the *Pentateuch* (or the "Torah" by the Jews – which means "Law"). The Torah comprises Genesis and four other books, Exodus, Leviticus, Numbers, and Deuteronomy, which will be explored later. The deep history found in Genesis is interwoven with rich lessons that are applicable to one's life. The action of the stories in this book, from the Garden of Eden, the fall of man, to God's chosen people in sin and slavery, and hope for deliverance, clearly depicts a cycle of God's plan for man.

The teachings of salvation and new birth (often only thought of as being in the New Testament when Jesus hit the scene) began in the Old Testament – right from Genesis. The salvation process, from creation, fall, and redemption, can be described in the modern way as generation, degeneration, and regeneration, which is an intricate part of life. It is seen in all of nature's processes, either in plants, animals, or even in aspects of man's life. There is so much beauty and knowledge to take in from the book of Genesis, so hold on tight as you gain an understanding of God's divine design from the very beginning.

The History of Creation

The history of creation stretches one's mind as far as understanding God's thought processes, and it also leaves an undeniable warmth that stems from his love revealed in every verse. It helps you catch a glimpse at the answer to life's biggest question, "What's my purpose?". It paints the picture of creation in a completely new light, different from how other ancient texts or history fables described it. It shows creation for what it truly is: the existence of something from nothing.

God didn't just make; He *created*, and this can be deduced from the use of the Hebrew word "Bara" in the original text, which means to create, not just make or reform. Creation means bringing something to life that never existed in any other form. This act is unique to the person of God only. It is not born out of inferiority, accident, or chance but an intentional process that reveals and expresses God's nature.

To Life from Nothing – Genesis 1:1-31

In Genesis, you get to see the exceptional working of God's infinite power. In his creation of the world, He spoke, bringing into existence life and matter solely by the words of His mouth. The significance of this spoken word will be seen later in this chapter, but for now, delve into the *whys* of God's order of creation, the potential wisdom that can be gleaned from it, and its relevance in today's life.

• Genesis 1:1

It all began with the creation of the heavens and the Earth. The very first verse introduces the creative process involved in the birth of the world. The first three words, "In the beginning," show something profound. Although the actual date or time of the beginning is not known or recorded in the Bible, the focus is centered on the creation and the creator, emphasizing that God was there in the time of creation and was responsible for the creation. This gives more light to Jer. 10:16, which acknowledges God as the maker of all things. An understanding of this first verse is crucial as it sets the stage for the rest of all biblical events. After stating God as the pioneer of life and everything that exists, you are then introduced to the first recorded creation, heaven and Earth.

• Genesis 1, Verse 2

The next verse talks about the state of the world after God created it. There are many existing theories about Genesis 1, verse 2. Speculations have been made by some theologians that there was a world with form and structure before verse 2. They propose that something might have happened, possibly chaotic, that left the world in the formless and empty state as it was described in Genesis 2.

The arguments for their theory and against all others are based on a passage in the Bible in Isaiah 45:18, where the creation of the world is seen as a place formed and established to be inhabited and a place formed not in vain. Their arguments remain that if God had created the world in verse 1, He couldn't have created a world without form and void, and the scripture in Isaiah 45 serves as confirmation that, indeed, the world God created was one formed to be inhabited.

A deeper look also revealed that the Hebrew word used for the word "Void" in Genesis 1 is the same as the word used for the phrase "in vain" in Isaiah 45. It is then clearly seen in Isaiah 45, where God states that His creation was not made in vain.

A common concept that has spread since the inception of this idea is the "Gap theory." This theory strengthens the idea that there was a non-recorded chronological gap between the first verse of Genesis and the second. The discovery of old fossils, including fossils in extinction, is used to emphasize this theory, stating that these fossils belong to an existing time not recorded and the fact that something must have happened to the world to leave it in a structureless state. However, this theory can also be refuted when a keen look is taken at Rom 5:12, which clearly states that death came by Adam, meaning before Adam, there was no death. The presence of fossils means something died. This now leaves a question of how death can be before the existence of Adam, leaving this theory with holes that can not be explained. Regardless of the merit on which it is founded, the gap theory has unsuccessfully linked the existence of fossils to itself.

This inconsistency in facts now puts a dent in this theory. If death was absent before the fall of man and Adam came in verse 6, what became of the supposed world in between verses 1 and 2? Regardless of the merit the gap theory is founded upon, which is Isaiah 45:18, the theorists have been unable to use the discovery of fossils as further proof.

As you read on, you see the Bible describing the face of the deep as one covered with darkness. When you think of the word darkness, it can be seen as a form of resistance. Resistance to the move of the Holy Spirit, as you will see in the next line. The Spirit of God was present but would not move until the darkness was removed. Every time there needs to be some form of creation or re-creation, the Holy Spirit institutes it; He begins every work of birthing something new. The transforming of the world into something habitable and beautiful began when the Bible tells you, "... the Spirit of the Lord hovers over the face of the waters" – Genesis 1:2. The state of the world, in a simple word, was "Chaos," and the Holy Spirit needed to move upon it to move it from that fallen state to a state in which it is loved and appreciated.

• Genesis 1, Verses 3-5

Unlike later translations, the Hebrew version does a fantastic job of stating just how wonderful this creation was. It says, "Light be. Light was." There is no delay; the creation of light was instantaneous. For there to be order, light had to come. The importance of the coming of light first is seen further in 2 Cor 4:3-6. God called it forth by speaking. This shows that light outside of its physical concept has a spiritual dimension; it's not as you have come to know it. There was light and darkness long before the sun and moon were created, which are used today as the primary sources of light. When the new Earth and Heaven come, God alone will be the light, as there won't be any distinction in time, meaning no need for the sun or the moon. This is addressed in Rev 22:5.

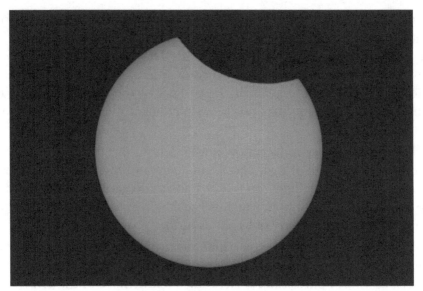

There will be no need for the sun or the moon in the new Earth and Heaven.'

- ### Genesis 1, Verses 6-8

Discussions have risen on whether the creation of the world was orchestrated in six literal days or if there is a deeper meaning indicating a time system different from the one acknowledged today. With no fixed conclusion on this or concrete show of proof, it's safe to go along with the six days as your regular time system.

With the presence of light, God goes on to create an atmospheric division. He says, "Let there be a firmament in the midst of the waters, and let it divide the waters from the waters."- Genesis 1:6. Thus, God made the firmament and divided the waters which were under the firmament from the waters which were above the firmament, and it was so." A firmament is seen as a space or an expanse, and with its creation, we see the waters above separated from the waters below. This shows that the water present on land was separated from those in the form of vapor in the sky.

- ### Genesis 1, Verses 9-13

The third day shows the creation of all vegetation as the dry land is divided from the waters. This shows that the whole Earth was covered with water at first, and the separation gave room for life to grow. It is also interesting to know that life started or existed before the supposed "sustenance of life" was formed. This means that this vegetation didn't have the sun for their sustenance but rather must have nourished themselves on the light of God created in verse 3. This verse has also raised a lot of discussions as people question the possibility of vegetative life thriving in the absence of celestial bodies. In contrast, others use this possibility to refute the claim that the world was created in eons (a very long time or an indefinite period) rather than days.

• Genesis 1, Verses 14-19

All creations of God are beautiful, and some might even say magical. In all of creation, the most talked about and researched about would be the creations of the fourth day. On the fourth day, God said, "Let there be lights in the firmament of the heavens to divide the day from the night; and let them be for signs and seasons, and for days and years, and let them be for lights in the firmament of the heavens to give light on the earth;" and it was so -Gen 1:14-15. Then God made two great lights: the greater light to rule the day and the lesser light to rule the night. He made the stars also. God set them in the firmament of the Heavens to give light on the Earth, and to rule over the day and the night, and to divide the light from the darkness, and God saw that it was good. So, the evening and the morning were the fourth day.

In contemporary times, the symbolism of the sun, moon, and stars holds diverse meanings for different people. Still, in all of these, one sure thing is that, as a Christian, these heavenly bodies were placed in the firmament to serve you for signs and seasons. For as long as possible, mankind has been known to make use of the sun, moon, and stars as a source of direction and for measurement of time.

In certain cultures, you will see the sun serving as a symbol of vitality, enlightenment, and even hope. In others, you will see the moon embody things like mystery, the cycles of life, and sometimes tranquility, but never really peace because when you look at John 14:27, it talks about God being the giver of true peace. Multiple symbolisms of the stars also exist today to represent guidance.

The Celestial bodies are still a wide topic today, as they not only influence people's belief systems, daily reflections, or artistic expressions but do so on a much grander scale. It has been said that the US government invested 100 million dollars in the study of extraterrestrial intelligence. Beyond all of this significance to the world, it shows you the excellence of God's power. If the sun had stood some miles closer to Earth than it does, it would have been catastrophic. The same could be said if it stood farther from the Earth. Still, God, in his infinite wisdom, knew the perfect spot, and at the end of this creation, we can see the creator himself, God, acknowledge that it was good. This helps reduce the argument of spontaneous Earth, as nothing left to chance is ever perfect.

- **Genesis 1, Verses 20-23**

The creation of the birds of the air and creatures of the sea shows the crafting of a God who is detailed, precise, and purposeful. By taking a deep look at the diverse species of creatures in the air and, most especially, the sea, some of which are yet to be discovered, you'll get to see the depth of complexity mirrored in His craftsmanship. This should also reveal to you God's interest in the little details of your life. His work is always thoroughly and meticulously done; take a look at the various breeds in existence within a single species. A Beagle will never look like a golden retriever, nor will a Siberian husky look like a bulldog, although they are all dogs.

The creation of the birds of the air and creatures of the sea shows the crafting of a God who is detailed, precise, and purposeful.[3]

- **Genesis 1: Verses 24-25**

A look at the fifth creation and then the first part of the sixth creation should leave anyone who comes across it in awe and amazement. You may wonder why; well, take a look at the giraffe and the platypus. God sure knows how to have fun with diversity. The platypus is an egg-laying, otter-footed, beaver-tailed, duck-billed aquatic creature that's commonly found in the waters of Australia. The male of the species is also known to be venomous, and they are one of the few mammals with venom. This is an animal with the features of a bird, a reptile, and a regular mammal.

There are several other animals like the platypus, but a core moral of the story, as seen on the fifth day of creation, is the commandment for them to come forth according to their kind. The constant reiteration of this commandment over time shows the importance of uniqueness to God. Although you will see different variations within one species, it stops or ends within the species. A dog evolving into a lion is yet to happen- it probably never will!

In today's world, there have been few success stories of cross-breeding between different species, and all of that has only strengthened the proof of God's commandments. This is seen in cases of a horse and a donkey with a hybrid called a "mule" or that of a lion and a tiger, which has given rise to hybrids called "liger" and "tigon." The making of these hybrids did not come without limitations - and there's one crucial limitation: A major characteristic of living things is the ability to reproduce and procreate, but this important function of any living thing is lacking in these hybrids as they are either infertile or incapable of mating with a fellow hybrid, showing an end to any continuation of such species.

This understanding tells you to be you at all times and only aspire to embody God's unique characteristics for you and not something else.

• Genesis 1, Verse 26

Although the creation of man took place on the sixth day as well, you must take a look at this separately, as the creation of mankind and the instructions given to him apply to you directly. The opening statement by God, to create man in His image, is worth focusing on, as it simplifies the question on the lips of most people, but definitely in the heart of everyone, which is "What's my purpose?" or "Why am I here?". A solid understanding ofverse26 will provide that answer. Verse 26 says you are created in God's image, and, at each point, He addressed himself in the plural form, explaining the concept of the Trinity, which is God the Father, God the Son, and God the Holy Spirit. This we know because they were present at the time of creation.

To understand who you truly are and why you are here, you must first know who created you. A knowledge of God is a knowledge of yourself. Life finds meaning and purpose when you know who created you and for what reason you were created. It's like staring into a clear stream or looking into a mirror; you are His replica, so when you see yourself, you see Him. Mankind alone has a different order from any other created being as only they possess a personality, spirituality, and conscience, which is their morality. Beyond this, they were also given the sole instruction and power to dominate. This is no coincidence; It is a consequence of being formed in His image. For this reason, His likeness is given to you as well.

The lessons in the story of creation are yet to be exhausted as fresh insights are being garnered daily. A continuous look into that chapter of the Bible will open you to new revelations that will influence your view on life and your everyday experiences.

The Garden of Eden: Adam and Eve

The Garden of Eden holds a lot of significance as it sets the stage for the events that played out later. Think of some of the most beautiful places in the world today: Machu Picchu, the Caribbean islands, Gobekli Tepe, etc. As beautiful as they are, they are nothing compared to the grandeur of the Garden of Eden. The Garden of Eden is much more than an oasis; it is a symbolic representation of the perfect harmony and beauty that should exist between God and mankind. It is a physical representation of our relationship with God, one of peace, love, joy, and unending happiness.

Adam and Eve in the garden of Eden.'

Moment of Reflection

1. What does the story of creation mean to you?

2. What are your thoughts on God's order of creation?

3. What aspects of God's creative process resonate with your personal beliefs or values?

4. How does knowing that you were created in the image of a supreme God influence your mind?

5. How do you view nature and other forms of life all around you in light of the story of creation?

6. After studying the lives of Adam and Eve, would you say you are like them in some ways?

7. When you think of what the Garden of Eden symbolizes, how do you relate it with what you understand perfection or paradise to be?

8. On topics like choices, temptation, and consequences, what lessons and insights did the story of Adam and Eve reveal on that?

9. Do you think you would have eaten the fruit if you were Eve? If yes, why? If No, why?

According to the Bible, the first-ever humans, Adam and Eve, were made on the sixth day of creation and placed in the garden to tend to it. From the creation story, upon mankind was the ability to dominate and subdue the Earth. At first, this was an instruction they continued without understanding. However, at the point of their temptation, they caved due to a lack of understanding, which reveals that deception is possible only in the face of ignorance. Although there are many other factors at play, the coming of the serpent to tempt Eve brought about the fall of man.

Chapter 2: Exodus and Liberation: Journeying with the Israelites

Walking through the genealogy of the Israelites and how they came to be in Egypt, you will find stories of Adam and Eve, Cain and Abel, Noah, Abraham and Sarah, Isaac and Jacob, and Joseph. The lives of these notable figures in Genesis shaped the frame for the next part of this adventure. The study of these lives reveals God's intentionality in bringing His promised people to a land He has prepared. Taking time to study the lives of each person mentioned above will also help in your understanding of the Bible as you progress, and you'll get to see God's method of dealing with His people.

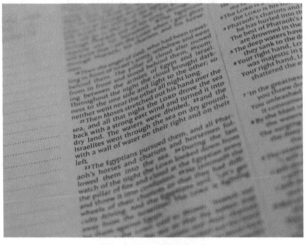

The book of Exodus.[5]

The story of the children of Israel in captivity under the rule of the Egyptians, their liberation, and their journey to the proposed promised land is one of great significance. A breakdown of the different timelines in the Bible would be incomplete without a detailed narration of the Israelites' journey. From the fulfillment of the prophecy, the exceeded time, the cry for help, the raising of a savior to deliver them, the processes of leaving, and the journey itself relates to the life of every individual, even in this present age. Here, you will learn lessons that will revolutionize your thought processes.

The Settlement

After the death of Joseph in Egypt, it seemed to the Israelites that their best days were behind them. However, from the previous chapter, one can easily deduce that God is completely intentional in His dealings and has a plan and set time for everything. The suffering and slavery of the Israelites in Egypt have been spoken of long before it happened.

In the time of Abraham, while he was yet called *Abram* in Genesis 15, God revealed to him that his descendants would be enslaved in a foreign land for four hundred (400) years. Although the prophecy stated 400 years, they remained in captivity for 430 years. There are many theories on why Genesis 15 says 400 years and 430 years were recorded in Exodus. One of these theories pins it on Moses' self-will to act before the set time when he killed an Egyptian. As of the time Moses killed the Egyptians, it was the 390th year, and they had ten more years until their liberation. Still, that act, which Moses might have seen as a way to help God or speed things up, was said to bring about the 30-year delay.

His actions towards the Egyptians led him to flee Egypt for the desert, where he stayed for 40 years until God visited him again. In today's modern age, the same is seen with most people; after getting a sense of God's will, they get so hasty to see it accomplished and fulfilled that they don't wait to find out God's method and pattern of accomplishing it, then messing it up in the process, or delaying it longer than anticipated. Learning to trust God wholeheartedly to see His will fulfilled in your life is key to growing your relationship with Him. When you take a look at Phil 1:6, you are reminded and assured that what He started, He most certainly can complete and not just complete, but also perfect in your life.

The Beginning of Liberation

The time God met Moses in the desert while he was tending to his father-in-law's sheep can be tagged as the start of the Israelites' freedom. Moses witnessed a bush that was ablaze but wasn't consumed. This incident shaped the rest of his life, as he later went on to deliver the children of Israel.

Moses being called by God before the burning bush.[6]

In the presence of God before the burning bush, something significant happened that many people overlook. God didn't begin to speak to Moses as soon the bush started to burn; He waited until He saw that Moses indicated an interest in the sight before him. Moses said, "I'll now turn aside and see this great sight, why the bush does not burn."- Exo. 3:3. Moses was definitely not a stranger to fire as he must have understood the concept of fire on a consumable material like the bush, but his first reaction was not fear or doubt; it was interest. This singular act signaled God to speak. It is not certain if Moses' words were said out loud or in his heart; the important thing was that God acknowledged it, and afterward, he received his assignment and the direction on how to carry it out.

Other noteworthy moments at the burning bush scene are:

1. **The Call of Moses' Name:** He called his name twice. God wanted to establish that he knew him, just as He knows you and everything that concerns you.

2. **The Holy Ground:** God instructed Moses not to draw near until he had taken off his shoes. This shows that God is Holy and will not associate himself with any form of filth. This means you are to approach Him in this manner, not necessarily taking off your shoes but with a consciousness that you are coming before a Holy God. It also shows how you should see yourself. Seeing that you were created in His image, you must not associate with anything that is regarded as filth by your heavenly father.

3. **God's Introduction:** This is crucial every time God speaks. He does not leave it up to chance for the recipient to deduce or decide who He is. He states that it may be known. Here, He introduces himself as the God of his fathers, which also shows a relationship and covenant that goes back long before Moses.

The Message: Moses didn't leave for Egypt empty; he left with a word. God told him to tell them, "I AM". A knowledge of your affiliations and associations always has a way of influencing your approach toward a new task. Knowing you don't have to do something alone always comes with a level of confidence. It gets better when you are working with someone reliable, trustworthy, powerful, and influential. He also went with a message for the Children of Israel in Exodus 3:15-17:

> *"Moreover, God said to Moses, 'Thus you shall say to the children of Israel: 'The LORD God of your fathers, the God of Abraham, the God of Isaac, and the God of Jacob, has sent me to you. This is My name forever, and this is My memorial to all generations.' Go and gather the elders of Israel together, and say to them, 'The LORD God of your fathers, the God of Abraham, of Isaac, and of Jacob, appeared to me, saying, 'I have surely visited you and seen what is done to you in Egypt; and I have said I will bring you up out of the affliction of Egypt to the land of the Canaanites and the Hittites and the Amorites and the Perizzites and the Hivites and the Jebusites, to a land flowing with milk and honey.'"*

The Ten Plagues

Upon arrival in Egypt, Aaron spoke to the Elders of Israel on behalf of Moses. Then Moses performed the signs God had instructed him to do, and this made the people believe. With God, you are told to believe by faith and not by sight, but humans are reliant on their senses. They often must see, feel, and smell before they can believe, and God knew this, which is why He enabled Moses to perform the signs. This shows that results often go further than just words, so you must strive to have results in all you do.

With the children of Israel in order, Moses and Aaron proceeded to the palace to speak to Pharaoh. Moses was already pre-informed by God that even with the signs he would show, He would harden Pharaoh's heart not to release the Israelites, and it happened just as God had said. He hardened the heart of Pharaoh so He could send the ten plagues to show both the Israelites and Egyptians that He was the only true God.

With the hardening of Pharaoh's heart came a backlash against the Israelites as their labor intensified and became more strenuous. This bred doubt in the hearts of the children of Israel as they questioned whether the God of their fathers truly sent Moses. It is common for people to embrace doubts and questions and then second-guess every belief once things seem not to go the way they pictured.

The First Plague: Water Becomes Blood

Despite the weak attempts of Pharaoh and his magicians to refute and rebut the signs of God, God's excellence and majesty shone through. Rather than having a change of heart, Pharaoh hardened further, just as God had said he would. This goes to show that only the Holy Spirit can fully bring someone to a place of spiritual illumination and clarity. The plagues were a show by God to bring to naught and ridicule the supposed prominence of the Egyptian deities. The first plague was to make a mockery of the Egyptian god, Hapi. This was the god of the Egyptian river Nile, who was worshiped for his supposed gift of natural fertility to his followers. From verse 14, God, working through Aaron, turned the Nile River into blood, so the Egyptians had to dig the earth to source fresh water. God wasn't done, so He made it possible for Pharaoh's magicians to be able to replicate that act to some degree, and his heart was further hardened.

God turned the Nile River into blood to mock the Ancient Egyptians' god of the Nile, Hapi.[7]

The Second Plague: Multiplication of Frogs

This next plague was a judgment against the Egyptian goddess of birth, Heqet, who was frog-headed. In ancient Egypt, frogs were revered and considered sacred. They represented symbols of generation and fertility. This god and her supposed powers were made a public joke as God caused the Nile to bring forth frogs that invaded every nook and cranny of Egypt aside from the dwelling place of the Israelites. They entered the Egyptian homes and took up all of their space, and when the frogs died, their bodies filled with stink were heaped up in huge piles all over the nation. It is exciting to read it the way the Bible puts it. The author of Exodus did not mince his words. No one was to be left out in Egypt, from their top-ranking officials to the lowest servants; frogs invaded everyone's personal space until they were losing their minds!

The Third Plague: Gnats

God took it up a notch in the third plague as the magicians of Egypt couldn't replicate it and openly declared before Pharaoh, "This is the finger of God. – Exo. 8:9" The third plague was a judgment against the deity Seth, who is the Egyptian god of the desert. God released gnats into all the land, displaying His sovereignty over sorcery and magic. The original Hebrew text did not say if these insects were gnats, but the Bible interpreted it to mean either gnats, lice, or some other type of insect, as the word used in the original text meant small insect. The acknowledgment of the magicians showed that they knew this was not just a natural phenomenal occurrence but rather the workings of a higher power. Regardless, Pharaoh's heart was still hardened.

The Fourth Plague: Swarm of Flies

Next came the flies, and there was a clear distinction between the land where the Israelites dwelled, Goshen, and the lands inhabited by the Egyptians. The Bible describes the plague as a grievous swarm of flies, and they terrorized the Egyptians without fail to the point at which Pharaoh sought out the help of Moses with a promise to let the children of Israel go. However, as you get to read the coming chapters in the Bible, you'll realize that Pharaoh didn't keep his promise. This plague was a judgment brought on Uatchit, the god of flies. God rains down judgment on the so-called gods of the Egyptians to show Pharaoh and his people that there is only one true living God.

The Fifth Plague: Death of Livestock

After the fourth plague ended, Pharoah went back on his promise to let the children of Israel go. The fifth plague was brought against two Egyptian gods, who were both depicted as cattle, the god Apis and the goddess Hathor. God, through Moses and Aaron, caused the death of all livestock belonging to the Egyptians, bringing no harm to those of the children of Israel. This shows God's steady hand of protection over those who choose to obey him. This is not just protection but an all-around provision for His Children. Matt. 5:45 talks about God causing rain to fall and the sun to shine on both the just and unjust, but it gets better for those who choose to acknowledge Him as Father and Lord.

The Sixth Plague: Boils

The boils of the sixth plague were intense. It is recorded in the scriptures that the magicians of Egypt could not stand before Pharaoh because they were also inflicted with the same affliction as all the other Egyptians. This significantly showed that the help the Egyptians had, or thought they had, from the magicians failed. This is applicable to daily living as well. However, it's not wrong to rely on others; there's a limit to the help they can offer, but when working with God, there are no fears of being left alone because He always comes through.

The Egyptian gods Sunu, Sekhmet, and Isis were the focus of the sixth judgment. These gods represented health, wellness, and disease, so boils were brought to make a mockery of their supposed power.

The Seventh Plague: Hail

God sent a message to Pharaoh beforehand to prepare him for this plague, and still, his heart remained hardened, just as God had said. God made it known that He was God, and there was none like him on all the earth. God also informed Pharoah that His presence on the throne was because of him, but he took it for granted. The hail brought judgment on Osiris, Set, and Nut, the gods of crop fertility, storm, and sky, respectively. So disastrous was the hail that it came with fire, destroying everything left in its wake. God went as far as warning Pharaoh to bring in and store everything alive as the hail would wipe them all out. At this point, division arose among the Egyptians. Some, in fear, went ahead and heeded the words of God through Moses by bringing in their servants, crops, and livestock in the field, while others refused, and hail came and consumed everything left outdoors.

The Eighth Plague: Locust

Locusts were brought upon the Egyptians, and all the late-season crops, like wheat and spelt, which were left behind after the barley was taken, were eaten up by the locust. Their gods, Osiris and Nut, were ridiculed and judged here, showing God's power. Just as He told Moses, His children would be able to tell their children of His power they witnessed and the diverse signs they saw.

The Plague of Locusts.[8]

The Ninth Plague: Darkness

The intensity of the darkness of the ninth plague was so much that the darkness was described as something that could be felt. It was judgment brought upon the god of light or the sun god, Re or Amon-Ra. Pharaoh himself was the symbol of this god. To the Egyptians, the sun's rising and setting signified life and death, meaning that whenever the sun rose in the morning, it meant life to the ancient Egyptians. When it set, it meant death. Similar to the third and sixth plagues, this plague came without any warning, isolating the Egyptians not only from the Israelites but also from themselves. The scripture says that no one could move from the point they were because of the severity of this plague.

By God taking over and subjecting unearthly darkness on their land, He was declaring ultimate supremacy over every other god, bringing the Egyptian top god into judgment and confining him to the realm of death. It only makes sense with this understanding that the plague of death would come next.

The Tenth Plague: Death of the Firstborn

The death of the firstborns meant and represented a lot. Firstly, firstborns are known to represent new beginnings, pride, hope, and joy; the death of the firstborns shows that this was taken away from the Egyptians. As the Bible describes it, "... great wailing would be heard from them" (Exodus 11:6) at the time that plague would come. Here comes the contrast: in the city of Goshen, the dwelling place of the Israelites, there was total serenity and tranquility; as God said, not even a dog would bark.

A deeper meaning also lies in the dog illustration used, as this final plague also brought judgment on the Egyptian god of the dead or the embalming god, Anubis, depicted as a dog.

This final plague also brought judgment on the Egyptian god of the dead, Anubis.[9]

This reveals God's deliverance and salvation that brings a peace no one can understand - as seen later in the New Testament in Philippians

4:7. The death of the firstborns pushed Pharaoh to let the children of Israel go, just as God had said. The Israelites adhered to all the instructions God gave them on their exit from Egypt and caused them to be favorably disposed towards the Egyptians, and they plundered the land, leaving with great spoils.

Road to Freedom

There was immense joy and excitement for the Israelites as they began their journey through the wilderness, but this joy was short-lived, as, after a while of journeying, the Egyptians went after them. Pharaoh's heart and that of his servants hardened towards the children of Israel, and they regretted letting them go and pursued after them in hopes of getting them back. However, God showed up again for His people; He drowned the Egyptians when He parted the Red Sea through the rod of His servant Moses. This singular act holds so much significance today for believers as it indicates complete salvation and total deliverance from any oppressor. God didn't leave anything up to time and chance but rather settled the matter once and for all, declaring total freedom for His people.

Moment of Reflection

1. Which of the ten plagues impressed you the most, and why?
2. The Children of Israel reacted to the increase in labor after Moses first met with Pharoah. What is usually your first disposition towards God when you face challenges? How do you gauge your faith in God based on your answer?
3. Based on God's dealings with the Israelites and the Egyptians, how do you see the nature of God?
4. Write down two characteristics of God that He displayed in the book of Exodus, and think about how these characteristics can affect your life.

God is very precise and intentional about everything He does. This is seen in how He meticulously arranged and ordered the ten plagues. When God works, He works on all fronts, never leaving any stone unturned. Any victory in God is always total victory!

Chapter 3: The Wisdom of Psalms and Proverbs: Guidance for Everyday Living

The "Fear of the Lord" is the core concept of the Bible, and all the teachings and exhortations you will find are centered around it. This concept is very much emphasized in the book of Psalms and Proverbs, with the theme focused on "Wisdom" and "Worship" more than any other book. Life as a Christian is meant to be lived in total worship of God through His wisdom, which makes these books so fascinating. A study of the book of Psalms will leave you in complete awe and reverence of God. It puts your heart in a posture of gratitude and worship primarily for God's role as your Creator, Father, Helper, and so much more. At the same time, the book of Proverbs teaches you how to live a life that pleases God. It addresses key areas of your life and will equip you with the wisdom to go about them. Aside from the book of Genesis, another good place to begin the study of the Bible would be the books of Psalms and Proverbs.

The book of Psalms.[10]

These are the only two books known to have multiple authors. The rich experiences of the different authors make for an amazing overlay of the chapters in these books. However, of all these authors, two stand out: King David of the Book of Psalms and King Solomon, King David's son of the Book of Proverbs.

When in doubt, joy, fear, excitement, pain, love, anguish, despair, faith, etc., these books will help to guide your heart. There is always a passage to address your current needs, give you insight, and uplift your spirit. They address all your emotions and provide you with instructions for righteous living. Below are many insights and key themes of this book.

Psalms: A Harmony of Hearts and Hymns

The book of Psalms is the expression of a man's heart. At any point in his life, it shows his connection to one source: God. This book is a compilation of songs; each lyrical poem is a revelation of the human heart in worship of God. Some of the authors of these songs in Psalms are mentioned at the start of the song in that chapter, while the authors of others are not. Some of the authors include King David, who wrote the most by authoring seventy-three (73) chapters, Moses, Aspha, the descendants of Korah, King Solomon, Herman the Ezrahite, and Ethan.

The book fully represents the meaning of its name, Psalms, which means "Praise" or "Songs of Praise," or its original name, which is the Hebrew word "Tehillim," meaning "Praise songs." It is composed of reflections, meditations, instructions, prayers for help, thanksgiving songs, hymns, corporate prayers for help, etc. Regardless of the other different genres seen in Psalms, its central focus is the praise and worship of God.

The book of Psalms spans nearly a thousand years, from the time of Moses to the post-exilic season in Babylon. Aside from being the longest book in the Bible and covering a diverse range of topics from creation, God's salvation, judgment, the kingdom of God, Israel's history, the law of life, the mystery of human conditions, and so much more, it is also the most read book of the Old Testament. It contains a total of 150 lyrical compositions that explore man's relationship with God, whether a celebration of victory, a cry for help, a search for comfort in trials, or a pouring out of one's soul in prayers.

In Matthew 22: 37, Jesus' teaching tells everyone that the greatest commandment is to love the Lord your God with all your heart, all your soul, and all your mind. A Christian in true pursuit of carrying out this commandment will turn to the book of Psalms, as it shows how to love God with total courage, consciousness, and intellect.

Proverbs: Wisdom Snapshots

In slight contrast, the book of Proverbs, attributed largely to King Solomon, beyond its wise sayings, provides insight into how to live. Although there are other authors involved in the compilation of this book, King Solomon serves as the principal author, having written a significant portion. He is renowned for his wisdom and wrote over 3,000 proverbs and over 1,005 songs. He was the third King of Israel after the era of judges when the Israelites had settled in Cannan. He ascended the throne at an early age after his Father, King David, died. Still, in his young and inexperienced state, he did something extremely wise for which he was rewarded greatly by God.

In a bid to seek help on how to lead God's people, Solomon offered a huge sacrifice to God, which led to God asking him to name whatever he wanted. Solomon asked for wisdom on how best to rule and lead God's people. This singular request pleased God, and He gave him his heart's desire and included everything else: wealth, fame, and peace from his enemies. This action gave Israel its longest reign of peace, which was 40 years without conflict or strife with other nations.

Solomon poured out this wisdom in the book of Proverbs. This book is characterized by practical advice on how to live a righteous and fulfilling life. It is so great that its teachings are not limited to those of a certain demographic, race, ethnicity, nativity, or class. Its teachings are so instrumental to life that they resonate with all who seek it out.

Proverbs covers a wide array of subjects vital for everyday living, like the importance and power of words, the value of pursuing knowledge and understanding, why it's important to conduct oneself ethically, how to make sound decisions, how to foster good relationships, stop a bad habit, learn a good habit, have an understanding of the principles that define a life laid out in total reverence to God, etc. You can always find something helpful in proverbs, and its insights are presented in nuggets, short and memorable, for easy assimilation and remembrance.

Inasmuch as this book shows the wisdom of life during the time of King Solomon, its value has not at all depreciated; it is still very much applicable in your everyday life today. The primary purpose of the book of Proverbs is to show you the path to wisdom, which is through the fear of the Lord. This is confirmed in the constant usage of the phrase "the fear of God" within the pages, more than any other book in the Bible.

An amazing feature you will notice as you study the book of Proverbs is its beauty in communicating this wisdom to its readers through the use of discourse and personification. It reveals a balance between man's choices and God's laws, showing how the sovereignty of God can harmonize with the free will of man. A conclusion you are bound to draw from your study of this book is that true wisdom can only be attained when a man is right with God, and that is the central focus of Proverbs. From Proverbs' perspective, a knowledgeable, smart, and intelligent man without God is devoid of wisdom.

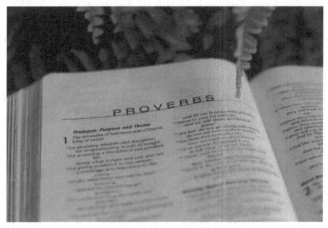

The book of Proverbs.[11]

Psalms and Proverbs: The Interlink

These two books, although distinct, offer complementary views or perspectives on key subjects of life, faith, and wisdom. Psalms consist primarily of poetic expressions of praise, lament, and worship, while Proverbs is more in line with practical wisdom. These different writing styles communicate similar messages. You will get to see how the insights highlighted repeatedly in these books are vital for your everyday living and how they resonate with the challenges faced in today's modern world.

A look at the historical and cultural context of Psalms and Proverbs reveals their enduring appeal. The book of Psalms, penned centuries ago, opens you up to the evolving societal and religious shifts seen in ancient Israel. Chapter by chapter, you will see how it successfully captures the triumphs, tragedies, and spiritual yearnings of the nation of Israel. This serves as a testament to man's eternal pursuit of connection with the divine. In comparison, Proverbs, which is often attributed to the time of the reign of King Solomon, immerses you in the wisdom of the ancient near East traditions. Proverbs' aphorisms and emphasis on practical wisdom are short and to the point, which differs from the expressive style of psalms. Culturally, the influence of the teachings in Psalms and Proverbs transcends the boundaries of religion alone. It cuts across a myriad of other fields, such as literature, philosophy, art, music, etc., throughout diverse cultures. The universal and enduring nature of their themes has served as wellsprings of inspiration for countless philosophers, writers, literature experts, artists, etc., across the expanse of human history. The way emotions are explored in these two books, especially Psalms and the pragmatic dispensation of insights in Proverbs, resonates universally, serving as a bridge for the gaps that exist among people from varied backgrounds, proving relevant in the different cultural and religious landscapes.

Beyond the artistic and cultural impact of Psalms and Proverbs, they have become subjects of profound inquiry by many scholars. Theological luminaries, Biblical scholars, and literary critics have engaged in a comprehensive examination of these texts, coming at them from various perspectives to unveil their different dimensions, both historical, literary, and theological. This interdisciplinary approach will not only deepen your comprehension of Psalms and Proverbs but will also illuminate their contextual significance. The scholarly interpretations stretch far beyond the confines of academia, providing you with insights that render these ancient texts not only accessible but profoundly relevant to contemporary issues and concerns. As a result, Psalms and Proverbs continue to serve as beacons of wisdom, guiding modern audiences such as yourself through the intricate terrain of this life with timeless and universal applicability.

Thematic Look at Psalms and Proverbs

Much has been said about the immense impact of the books of Psalms and Proverbs in your life today. In this section, we look at some of the key themes which are a part of everyday life.

Wisdom in Adversity

Adversity in life is not a new concept. Just as there are days of prosperity, days of adversity are just around the corner. This is not a shot at pessimism; it's how the world works. It is expressed in the story of the seven years of abundance and want during the time of Joseph in Genesis 41. One of each is always bound to happen at any given point in a man's life. Your question should be, what does God's word have to say about His children in the days of adversity, and what wisdom can be gleaned from these books for such times?

You will experience adversity, but you should never be afraid.[12]

The Bible makes it clear that as a Christian, you will experience adversity, but you shouldn't worry, be afraid, or cower; rather, you should be courageous because Christ Jesus, your Lord, has overcome the world. It is with this understanding that you draw your victory. This is seen in John 16, verse 33, and Proverbs instructs believers about adversity. In verse 10 of chapter 24 in Proverbs, you are encouraged to persevere always and be strong in the day of adversity, meaning it will come, but your approach to it will determine how you come out of it- victorious or defeated. This verse teaches you to be resilient and determined when you are confronted with different challenges.

Similarly, this understanding is stretched further in Psalms. For example, various passages like Psalm 34, verses 17-18, show the author expressing a deep emotional response to adversity but not losing heart. Rather than fret in the face of adversity, their cry is turned towards their helper, God. He hears them and provides comfort to them from their troubles. The beauty of Psalms is that it doesn't shy away from the pain experienced during tough times; neither does it dwell on it solely. Instead, it acknowledges the struggle while relying on a higher power, God, for strength and deliverance.

This approach to adversity is just as effective today. Instead of wallowing in fear and doubt, which breeds depression in the face of challenges, you should draw wisdom from Psalms and Proverbs by turning to God for strength to help you sail through victoriously with joy. It's just like the story of a man called Job in the Bible, whom Satan tormented with a great adversary to get him to turn away from God and lose faith. However, Job reacted in one of the most impressive ways possible: When he lost all he had, he said, "... the Lord gives, and the Lord takes. Blessed be the name of the Lord – Job 1:21". So, you see, it's possible to be joyful even amid distress. Notice the word joyful and not happy: Happiness is a result of the physically pleasurable things around you, while joy stems from an inner peace from God not influenced by your surroundings or circumstances.

Challenges indeed differ from person to person, but the primary method of victory is the same for everyone: turn to God, draw strength, approach the challenge in Faith with joy, and enjoy your victory. Psalm 34:19 and Proverbs 3:5-6 also shed further light on a Christian's idea of adversity, "The righteous person may have many troubles, but the LORD delivers him from them all" and "Trust in the LORD with all your heart and lean not on your understanding; in all your ways submit to him, and he will make your paths straight." Together, these books offer a comprehensive view of facing adversity with a combination of practical wisdom from Proverbs and the emotional and spiritual perspective found in Psalms. It is a holistic approach that encourages both mental fortitude and spiritual reliance during challenging times.

The Power of Words

Proverbs 18:21 says, "Life and death are in the power of the tongue." This verse encapsulates everything you would read in this whole section. It highlights the impact that the words you say can have on your life. There are no limits to how far your words can go or how deep into the nooks and crannies of your life they can reach. This verse also underscores the responsibilities that come with speaking and your ability to communicate, urging you to be careful in your usage of words.

A similar discussion on the power of words is also seen in Psalms in its usual poetic form. In Psalms 141:3, the Psalmist makes a plea to God, asking him to set a guard over his mouth and to keep watch over his lips. Although in a different style to Proverbs, it has a similar message. With the infusion of emotions, you can sense the desperation of his words as you read, which shows his understanding of the power of words.

Proverbs 16:24 says, "Gracious words are a honeycomb, sweet to the soul and healing to the bones." in Proverbs 15:4, "The soothing tongue is a tree of life, but a perverse tongue crushes the spirit." This imagery vividly contrasts the life-giving power of gentle, comforting words with the destructive force of harsh, hurtful speech. A read through Psalms and Proverbs highlights the profound influence of words in all aspects of your life. You are urged to wield your words with care, knowing the weight it carries. When you align your speech to bring life, you are pleasing God and working in the fear of Him.

Gracious words are compared to the sweetness of honeycomb in the book of Proverbs.[18]

Pursuit of Righteousness

A pursuit of righteousness is synonymous with an honorable and flourishing life. Still, outside its numerous benefits, it is a call to all

Christians. Proverbs 21:21 tells you that "Whoever pursues righteousness and love will find not only life but prosperity and honor." The book of Psalms not only addresses the topic of righteousness multiple times, but this discourse sets the tone for the book in general. The first three verses of the Psalm talk about the lifestyle of a man living in righteousness and not pursuing ungodliness.

Psalm 1:1-3 says,

> *"Blessed is the man that walketh not in the counsel of the ungodly, nor standeth in the way of sinners, nor sitteth in the seat of the scornful. But his delight is in the law of the Lord; and in his law doth he meditates day and night. And he shall be like a tree planted by the rivers of water, that bringeth forth his fruit in his season; his leaf also shall not wither; and whatsoever he doeth shall prosper."*

In this verse, the concept of righteousness is connected to a life deeply rooted in God's word; such a life always results in productivity, stability, and prosperity. Choosing to be honorable is always vital to the life of a believer walking with God. It might seem easier to alter the numbers at work, cheat on a test, tell a lie, or gossip about a friend, but these things do not align with your principles as a believer, so they shouldn't be found in or around you.

Furthermore, Proverbs 11:19 provides a contrast between the outcomes of righteousness and wickedness: "Truly the righteous attain life, but whoever pursues evil finds death." This close comparison points out the transformative impact of choosing the path of righteousness. In comparison with Psalms, Psalm 34:15 echoes this sentiment when it says, "The eyes of the Lord are on the righteous, and his ears are attentive to their cry." You receive this assurance that reflects God's divine connection with you as you earnestly pursue righteousness.

Expanding on the pursuit of righteousness, Proverbs 21:3 states, "To do what is right and just is more acceptable to the Lord than sacrifice." This verse emphasizes the intrinsic value of righteous actions over external rituals. It's never really about the nice things you say; the posture of your heart matters more to God, as you can see within this verse. This also relates to a chapter in Psalms that asks the question, "Who is fit to inquire of God and who is fit to live on his Holy Mountain"- Psalm 15:1. The answer then goes on to describe the characteristics of a righteous man as one who fits the bill in this context.

Righteousness is a path that leads to life. As you study the books of Psalms and Proverbs, you will discover more verses that touch on this topic, giving you a better understanding of righteousness. This pursuit is an active, intentional journey towards the right and just thing in the sight of God. Psalm 119:1-2 says, "Blessed are those whose ways are blameless, who walk according to the law of the LORD. Blessed are those who keep his statutes and seek him with all their heart."

Moments of Reflection

1. If you were asked to mention the one thing you desire the most now, just like Solomon, what would it be?

2. Psalms often explore a range of emotions, from joy to sorrow. Which Psalm do you find most relatable to your current feelings or life situation? Why?

3. Reflect on a mistake or lesson learned in your life. How does the concept of learning through mistakes, emphasized in Proverbs, resonate with your experiences?

4. Proverbs offer practical wisdom for daily living. What proverbial advice do you find particularly relevant to a current situation or decision you're facing? How might applying this wisdom impact your choices?

One thing is guaranteed: a study of the books of Psalms and Proverbs will leave you better than it found you. You have the assurance of a renewed way of thinking. You can begin to take actionable steps from the lessons of these books that reshape your choices and habits.

Chapter 4: The Life and Teachings of Jesus

Learning about the life of Jesus and His teachings is beyond the purpose of acquiring knowledge. It guides your understanding of God and reveals His heart about life's purpose, which in turn causes a total transformation in your heart. These stories and teachings are not time-bound, as their lessons are still very relatable in today's contemporary world. It doesn't matter if you're starting on your Bible

The birth of Jesus.[14]

journey; a view into Jesus' life and teachings will give you a new perspective of life, fill your heart with the boldness to face trials and challenges, and equip you with faith and expectation for His promised end to all His Children. As you go into the pages of this chapter, get ready to yearn for a deeper relationship with God.

The Birth of Jesus

The birth of Jesus is so significant that every event, story, and teaching right from the start of Genesis, all through the books of the Old Testament into the New Testament, were preparations for the coming of the Messiah, Jesus. The prophecies of His birth and life have been recounted centuries before His arrival. You can consider the manifestation of His birth as a collision of the supernatural and natural, an event divinely orchestrated by God. It all began with Mary, a young virgin woman engaged to a man in the small town of Nazareth, who finds favor in the sight of God and receives a visit from an angel. The angel came with the news of her being chosen to bear the savior of the whole world, the son of God. Can you stop to imagine Mary's possible thoughts and reactions to such news?

However, another person who really mattered was her fiancé, Joseph, and God made it possible for him to stay by her side as this miracle unfolded. He was also visited by an angel and instructed by God not to put Mary away but to stay with her because the child was from the Holy Spirit.

In Luke chapter one, Mary, still in the process of coming to terms with this divine revelation, paid a visit to her relative, Elizabeth, who was heavily pregnant. This visitation had more significance than simply two relatives paying each other visits. During this visit, the baby in Elizabeth's womb, whom you will know to be John the Baptist, filled with the spirit of God right from the womb, instantly recognized the presence of His Lord, Jesus, in the womb of Mary and leaped for joy. Understanding the sign, Elizabeth recognizes the significance of Mary's role in the grand scheme of God's divine plan.

Around the time of the conception of Jesus in chapter 2 of Matthew, the Bible spoke about three wise men who can be regarded today as scholars or astronomers. These wise men coming from the east were said to receive a sign from a star and chose to follow that star, leading them to Judea. Coming from a long distance across vast landscapes, they sought the King whose star they saw appear one night, and it led them to Jesus.

The birth of Jesus in a manger is beyond the result of an earthly activity; it wasn't just the by-product of an overcrowded inn during a tax census. The simplicity of the stables was an indication of God's humility to take on the form of man and His willingness to become human to help men right their wrongs. The birth of Jesus wasn't merely a historical event; the lessons from Mary's courage, the wise men's journey, the political turbulence, and Joseph's faith all sum up the reality of the supernatural.

Meanwhile, on the political stage, Herod, the ruler of Judea, learned of the birth of a king through the wise men and felt a threat to his position as King. In Matthew 2, Herod issued a decree that all male children under the age of two born in Bethlehem were to be killed due to the threat posed by the birth of Jesus.

The Miracles of Jesus

After His birth, Joseph, being warned by an angel in a dream, fled with Mary and Jesus to Egypt until the death of King Herod. However, in fear that Herod's son might continue in the footsteps of his father, Joseph didn't return to Judea but moved to the land of Galilee, to the small city of Nazareth, where Jesus grew up until the start of His ministry at the age of 30. From His conception in a humble stable to His studies at the temple with the scholars when He was 12, and up until his baptism by John at the age of 30, the Bible recorded that Jesus grew in wisdom and favor. When the time came for Him to step into the forefront of public life, in the fulfillment of the will of God upon Him, He began to do remarkable things. Jesus performed diverse miracles, some of which will be discussed here and others you will come to know about as you go deeper into your study of God's word.

You must understand just how extraordinary His signs were in a time when the multiple factors at play were physical ailments, political turbulence, and economic challenges. The coming Messiah was their only beacon of hope. Just like Herod, they all thought that being the promised Messiah, Jesus was coming to free them from Roman rule and rule them as a king, but Jesus had far better plans. His presence was to offer them hope, far beyond their present struggles, and a life of freedom, then and after, to all who accepted Him.

All through the four gospels, you will find Jesus healing the sick, as many came to Him for healing. This act was not just a show of power but rather Jesus' sincere response to the cries of His people in desperate need of restoration, as they were in a parlous situation with the Romans. As Jesus walked among the people, turning water into wine, multiplying loaves and fishes, and even raising the dead, you will see a great significance in each of those acts. It wasn't just about the magnificence of the miracles but the recipients of these miracles. Every person in each miracle was just a regular individual going about their lives with their daily struggles, hoping for some sort of deliverance. Jesus came at the right time when they were desperately in need of a miracle.

Feeding of the Crowd

One of the extraordinary feats accomplished by Jesus was the feeding of the five and four thousand. This account of the multiplication of fish and bread was recorded in four books of the Bible: Mattew, Mark, Luke, and John. In this particular experience, Jesus, while teaching, was moved with compassion for the crowd, as they had been with Him for three days in the wilderness without anything to eat. Not wanting to send them home on an empty stomach, Jesus resolved to feed them. However, His disciples informed Him that only five loaves of bread and two fishes were available. Jesus was not moved by the insignificant quantity of food in comparison to the number of persons present. He asked that the disciples make the people sit in a particular order, took the bread and fish, and gave thanks to God. After Jesus had finished, He gave it back to His disciples to distribute to the people, and there was more than enough to go around. The five loaves of bread and two fishes were successfully distributed among five thousand people who ate their fill, with twelve baskets of food left over.

Jesus feeding five thousand people.[15]

This miracle revealed that Jesus wasn't only interested in the spiritual growth of His people, as He had done for the past three days. He was also interested in their physical needs as well. It also showed His divine power over scarcity as a symbol of God's supernatural abundance.

Turning Water to Wine

Another amazing miracle was at a wedding feast, where Jesus turned water into wine. Jesus was present at a wedding in Cana, and the wine being used for guests ran out while the wedding was still in full swing. This led those present to seek help from Mary, Jesus's mother, on what to do. Knowing who her son was, she brought it up to Him, although Jesus revealed it wasn't time for Him to perform such manifestations. However, being moved with compassion, He instructed the servants to fill up six empty stone jars with water and serve them to the guests. They heeded Jesus' instruction, and the water in the jars became wine. The guest acknowledged that the wine was better than the first batch that was served when they asked, "Why have you saved the best for last?" (It was customary to serve the best wine first at any gathering, so when the guests were drunk with the good wine, they would not be able to tell the difference!)

Jesus turned water into wine.[16]

This event is considered Jesus' first public miracle, which symbolizes His divine authority over even the elements of nature. The abundance and quality of the wine produced in this miracle also show Jesus' ability to bring about joy and richness even in the most unexpected situations.

The Woman with the Issue of Blood

This Bible revealed the struggle of a woman who had lived with a particular condition for twelve years and had spent all her money on non-profitable visits to physicians, yet it continued to worsen. While in the middle of her pain from the bleeding, she hears of Jesus and, in faith, goes to Him for her healing. The beautiful thing about this miracle was the absence of Jesus laying His hands on her; rather, she was healed by her faith, which was clearly displayed in her actions. She believed all she had to do to get her healing was to touch Jesus' cloak. Not minding the pressure from the crowds around Jesus, she pressed until she reached the hem of Jesus' garment. As she touched the garment, the bleeding dried up instantly, and it was recorded that Jesus immediately knew that virtue had gone out of Him. After Jesus had found her in the crowd, He was impressed by her level of faith and declared that her faith had made her well in Mark 5:34: "Daughter, your faith has made you well; go in peace and be healed of your disease."

This miracle illustrates Jesus' compassion towards the sick, His willingness to respond to faith, and His power to heal. It also emphasizes the importance of faith and persistence in seeking a miracle.

These miracles and many more contributed to the spread of His fame across the land - tales of a man who defied the laws of nature, who brought relief to the sick, and who challenged the societal order. These were not just a series of events; rather, they were events that unfolded in response to the needs and challenges of the time in ancient Judea.

Jesus' Ministry and Teachings

The diverse miracles are not the only things noted about the life of Jesus. His teachings formed a core part of Christianity today, and it would be incomplete to look at the life of Jesus without buttressing the lessons He taught. There were no limits on the subjects covered in Jesus's teachings. He covered every area of life: salvation, the kingdom of God, faith, prayers, humility, money, possessions, love and compassion, repentance, forgiveness, judgment, the end times, etc. Either directly or through the use of parables, Jesus always gave vital life lessons. He came to show men how to live a purposeful life effortlessly. The trees on the earth, the fishes in the sea, and the birds of the sky don't struggle to thrive in their natural habitat, and that was what Jesus came to do, showing us how to live a life of total worship to God seamlessly, and this He communicated through His teachings.

Here are some of Jesus' teachings in Parables and the insights to be gleaned from them;

The Parable of the Good Samaritan

In this parable, Jesus tells the story of a man who was attacked by robbers on his way from Jerusalem to Jericho and solicited help from passersby, and none but one would help him. Jesus made us know that the only person who volunteered to help was a Samaritan, while the others who wouldn't stop to help were a Levite and a Jewish priest. This statement alone has great tribal significance. In those times, the Jews and Samaritans were enemies. The Samaritan laid him on his horse, took him to an inn, and paid for his medical bills. The lessons are clear: compassion knows no boundaries, regardless of tribe, race, ethnicity, nationality, etc. Love should always come first. Today, this parable challenges you to extend kindness and care to all, regardless of societal divisions or differences.

The Parable of the Prodigal Son

Jesus shares the story of a wayward son welcomed home by a loving father. A man had two sons, and his second son requested his inheritance, which he obliged. His son goes away and squanders his part of the inheritance and is left with nothing to the point of being willing to eat with the pigs. In that state of soberness, repentance, and reflection, the son returned home to his father. He begged to be taken back, even as a servant. The father welcomed him and held a feast in his honor.

The parable emphasizes God's unconditional love and forgiveness as a father to His children. Today, it serves as a reminder that, no matter your past, you can always return to the open arms of a forgiving and compassionate God who is ever ready to receive you.

The Parable of the Mustard Seed

In this parable, Jesus uses the analogy of a mustard seed to explain the importance and significance of humble or small beginnings. The mustard seed, when sown, is considerably small. Still, when given time, it grows into a large plant that contributes greatly to its environment. Jesus teaches about the Kingdom of God, which started small but flourished remarkably. The significance today lies in the transformative power of small acts and humble beginnings. It serves as a reminder that even the smallest efforts can have a profound impact.

The Parable of the Lost Sheep

In this parable, Jesus spoke of a shepherd who had a hundred sheep and lost one. Out of love for the one, he leaves the ninety-nine to find the one lost sheep. Some might consider it foolish, but it shows great love, especially when you see yourself as the one. It conveys God's relentless pursuit of each individual. Today, it serves as an encouragement to love and value everyone. Remember, no one is beyond redemption or unworthy of God's love.

The Parable of the Sower

In this parable, a sower went about sowing on a particular day. As he sowed, Jesus explained that the seeds fell on different grounds, by the wayside, among thorns, on stony grounds, and on good and fertile soil. Due to the different foundations of the seeds, they all ended differently. Birds ate up the ones by the wayside. The seeds among thorns sprang up but were choked by the thorns. Seeds on stony ground grew up fast, but because of inadequate depth of soil for a good foundation, the sun scorched the plants. Finally, the ones that fell on good and fertile ground thrived and produced a harvest thirty-, sixty-, and a hundred-fold!

Jesus used this metaphor of different soils to explain how Christians receive the word of God at different times. This parable teaches the importance of cultivating a heart that is always receptive to God's word. This parable should serve as a challenge to always strive for a heart that will bear lasting fruits.

The Crucifixion and Resurrection

The crucifixion and resurrection of Jesus will forever shape the course of history. In a time when the Romans ruled the Jews, there were many complexities surrounding religion, societal demands, and expectations. The use of crucifixion as a form of punishment was reserved for the most heinous of criminals because of how brutal it was. Following the weight of Jesus' ministry, He was bound to make some enemies, especially among people who were not pleased with His methods and teachings. They conspired and had Him arrested on the basis of many false allegations. Jesus, being innocent, faced the agony of the cross. Despite being the son of God, the Bible revealed that He wasn't immune to the pain and shame of the cross. This was demonstrated when Jesus was recorded praying to God that He may not face the judgment of the cross in the book of Matt. 26:39; "Father, if it's possible, let this cup pass from me; nevertheless, not as I will, but as you will." However, His crucifixion wasn't merely a cruel event of injustice among men and a challenge to the societal norms and religious expectations of that era. It was also a convergence of His divine sacrifice. Beyond the spiritual significance, it shows the harsh realities of Roman oppression and the great lengths the spiritual leaders of old were willing to go to preserve their beliefs.

Jesus's crucifixion shows his love for humanity.[17]

After facing the shame and wrath of crucifixion, Jesus was buried. However, just as prophecies of old revealed in Psalm 16:10, "For you will not abandon my soul in Sheol, or let your Holy One see corruption," Jesus rose again. This also confirms His words to His disciples when He told them in Mark 9:31 that "The Son of Man is going to be delivered into the hands of men. They will kill Him, and after three days He will rise". Jesus rose from the grave on the third day, defying death and ushering in a new life for all who believed. His triumph over the grave and death brought about hope and unspeakable joy to all who believed in Him.

The crucifixion and resurrection of Jesus first show His sacrificial love. Just as He said in John 15:13, "There is no greater love than this: that a person would lay down his life for the sake of his friends." This shows a love that goes beyond culture and time. The brutality of the crucifixion of the cross shows the weight of your sins and the great lengths Christ was willing to go to have you reconciled back to Him. The understanding of His sacrifice sheds more light on a Christian's hope beyond the challenges of life for an afterlife in eternity. This serves as the cornerstone of the Christian Faith.

Moments of Reflection

1. The Parable of the Prodigal Son is a powerful story of forgiveness and redemption. Is there any area of your life that makes you feel inadequate, imperfect, and detached from God, just like the Prodigal Son? What steps should you take following this parable?

2. From the parable of the Good Samaritan, who do you consider your neighbors to be, and is there anyone you need to extend a hand of compassion to today?

3. Do you believe that Jesus' life, death, and resurrection were for you? How can this reality affect your relationship with Him?

4. Jesus often emphasizes the importance of faith. Are you trusting God for something in your life right now? What actions are you willing to take to demonstrate your faith?

Exhausting the lessons of Jesus' life in a few pages would be impossible. To discover the many lessons and insights from the life of Jesus, His birth, miracles, teachings, trials, betrayal, cross, death, burial, and resurrection, you are encouraged to take on a personal in-depth study. Take your time studying the stories to unveil the truths and lessons they carry for your life. This is not an account of history but an invitation to the *more* that lies between the verses of the Bible – for a chance to experience a life of unending love and total victory found in Christ.

Chapter 5: Acts of the Apostles: The Early Church in Action

The story of the Apostles in the book of Acts follows the life of ordinary folks going about their daily activities but somehow encountering the most transformative experience that causes a noteworthy change in their lives and the world. They weren't superheroes or mystical beings but simply men living life: fishermen, carpenters, tax collectors, tent makers, etc. The change they had was due to the encounter they had with Jesus Christ after His resurrection. His arrival ushered in a new life for them that turned the world around. These were men like you, who started with uncertainty but chose to be guided by an unwavering faith in the One who called them and in whom they believed.

The change the Apostles had was due to the encounter they had with Jesus Christ.[18]

A spectrum of human expressions and emotions is revealed in this book when tracing key events in the lives of the Apostles: from faith to fear and back to faith again, joy, hope, and even moments of greed and anger. In essence, they were humans with normal human emotions but touched by the hand of God. The beauty of this book lies in God's seamless ability to make something great out of nothing. This chapter is meant to show you the hope that lies in yielding completely to God and encourage you to stay steadfast on the path while proclaiming the good news you have also received.

The Book of Acts Introduced

The book of Acts is attributed to the esteemed Apostle Luke, who also authored a Gospel named after him. It is recognized as a seamless continuation of his detailed narrative of the life of Christ. St. Luke the Evangelist penned the Acts of the Apostles in Greek, beginning from Christ's birth and extending through the early days of the Church. It is recorded that this book was composed between 70 CE and 90 CE and serves as a comprehensive account of the unfolding events within the burgeoning Christian community.

His style and manner of writing, seen in the Book of Acts, can be ascribed to his occupation. His care for the most minute things and his attention to detail transcended his role as a physician. It was seen in how he meticulously gave a detailed account of the early Church: the receiving of the Holy Spirit, the spread of the Gospel, Paul's conversion, etc. He was learned, and that added advantage helped him, through the inspiration of the Holy Spirit, to encapsulate even the experiences of others when he wasn't present at the happenings. Luke was believed to be of Greek descent, with some historians suggesting the possibility of him originating from Antioch in Syria, a province under Rome. However, both claims remain unclear. What remains unequivocal is that Luke's presence in Antioch resulted in a close companionship with Paul throughout his extensive missionary journeys. In one of Paul's letters, found in the book of Colossians, he affectionately addresses Luke as "the beloved physician." While Luke doesn't explicitly mention Paul by name, his use of the inclusive "We" in certain sections of the book of Acts strongly implies his direct participation in several pivotal events alongside Paul. Finishing what he started was important to him, as you will see in Acts 1:1-2, where he clearly stated to the recipient of the book of Acts, a man called

Theophilus, that it was only right, that after talking about the life of Jesus, from his birth to the day He was taking up, he also discussed the lives and roles of the early apostles in the spread of the Gospel. He was able to achieve that to a great degree, as he provided a well-researched record of events surrounding the growth of the early Christian community.

The presence of the Acts of the Apostles in the New Testament is vital for the full comprehension of the message it carries. The transition from Christ's coming and how His disciples took up. It shows the series of events from Christ's ascension to the coming of the Holy Spirit in the upper room; how people left in doubt, worry, and fear after Christ's death were filled with boldness and power at the coming of the Holy Spirit. Not having this as a part of the compendium of the New Testament would have made the entire book impossible to understand.

Pentecost: The Coming of Fire and Power

The Pentecost was initially a celebration of the Jews; it was a time when they were expected to gather with their families and rejoice before Jehovah, their God. They were to observe this celebration with a free-will offering in their hands to Jehovah. It was a one-day feast, which took place fifty days after the Passover. It was observed regularly by the Jews, with many pilgrims trooping in from all around to take part. Pentecost originated from the Greek word "fiftieth," traditionally referred to as the Harvest feast or the Feast of Weeks, and took on new meaning for believers in Acts chapter 2. Beyond its original significance, it is now seen as the birthday of the Christian Church, marking the transformative arrival of the Holy Spirit.

> "When the day of Pentecost arrived, they were all together in one place. Suddenly, a sound came from heaven like a mighty rushing wind, and it filled the entire house where they were sitting. Also, they received divided tongues as fire appeared to them and rested on each one of them. And they were all filled with the Holy Spirit and began to speak in other tongues as the Spirit gave them utterance." (Acts 2:1-4)

This event, as recorded in Acts 2, was a fulfillment of the prophecy given to prophet Joel in Joel 2:28-32 concerning Pentecost. This fulfillment of the prophecy becomes one of the reasons why Jesus asked them to wait a while in Jerusalem before going out to proclaim the gospel.

"And it shall come to pass afterward, that I will pour out my Spirit on all flesh; your sons and your daughters shall prophesy, your old men shall dream dreams, and your young men shall see visions. Even on the male and female servants in those days, I will pour out my Spirit. "And I will show wonders in the heavens and on the earth, blood and fire and columns of smoke. The sun shall be turned to darkness, and the moon to blood, before the great and awesome day of the LORD comes. And it shall come to pass that everyone who calls on the name of the LORD shall be saved. For in Mount Zion and Jerusalem, there shall be those who escape, as the LORD has said, and among the survivors shall be those whom the LORD calls." (Joel 2:28-32)

The event sets Christianity apart and is a unique and beautiful style of worship. It is considered superior to other religions because of a promise fulfilled—the presence of the Holy Spirit among the believers.

After the resurrection of Jesus, He did not ascend immediately. He stayed a while, talking to His disciples and strengthening their faith. In the midst of that, their hearts were stirred up to go out and preach the gospel, but the power and boldness they needed to confidently declare the good news was not yet with them, and this power was Jesus' promise to them, that they would receive only if they waited in Jerusalem. So far, from the Old Testament to the first four books in the New Testament, records of the Spirit of God have only been mentioned to rest upon the men in whom He found favor and not within them. However, this method of receiving the Holy Spirit totally changed. The disciples, following Jesus's instructions, waited in Jerusalem for ten days, a testament to their strong faith despite the absence of Jesus. This was remarkable, considering the fear they must have felt after their leader's brutal death. Instead of fleeing, a logical choice at the time, they stayed and waited. The outcome was the outpouring of God's Spirit on all present in the upper room.

In the first four books in the New Testament, records of the Spirit of God have only been mentioned to rest upon the men in whom He found favor and not within them.[19]

On the day of the Pentecostal ceremony, the apostles were all together praying. The Bible describes the coming of the Holy Spirit as a sound from heaven like that of a mighty wind rushing in one direction and filling up the space they were in, followed by the appearance of what was described as "Cloven tongues of fire" resting on each person present. Something even more strange and magnificent was the aftermath of the sound and fire. The disciples, with the help of the Holy Spirit, spoke in the languages of the different people present during the feast of harvest as a confirmation of His presence in them. What adds to the grandeur is that pilgrims gathered during the Pentecost, representing diverse languages. Despite this diversity, the disciples were heard by all in their respective languages. Some of the persons present thought the disciples to be drunk, but Peter, Jesus' disciple, who was once shy, now filled with so much confidence, boldly refuted their claim and confidently began to preach to all present. He spoke of how Jesus of Nazareth, whom they had crucified, is their foretold Messiah and the living Christ, the One who had conquered sin and death and is now seated victoriously on the right-hand side of God.

The People became remorseful, repented of their past deeds, and inquired of Peter what they should do. Peter led them to full repentance by telling them how they were to turn from their wicked ways, repent wholeheartedly, believe, and receive Jesus Christ as their Lord and personal savior. On that day, about three thousand were recorded to be saved and became a part of the body of Christ by the power of the Holy Spirit. Peter's teaching that day is considered one of the most important and powerful sermons in the whole of the New Testament. That moment ignited a fire that resulted in the spread of the Gospel among the Jews and beyond to the Gentiles.

Great significance lies in the study of the event on Pentecost, from the meaning of the loud sound heard from heaven to the flaming fire and its choice in shape, even to the utterance they received. However, two key significances that must be highlighted are the fulfillment of God's promise, which showed that God always keeps His word, and no matter how long it takes, we are encouraged to wait because it will surely come to pass, as seen in Habakkuk 2:3. The second would be the importance of the coming of the Holy Spirit. God did not send His Spirit to have you sitting down; He imbues men with power by His Spirit to do His will seamlessly. This is evident with Apostle Peter and the other Apostles, who cowered in fear a while ago, having received the Holy Spirit, and became bold enough to lead three thousand souls to salvation in a day. After the outpouring of God's Spirit, the apostles and all other followers of Jesus actively continued in the propagation and proclamation of the good news, which is God's love for the world.

The Spread of the Gospel among the Apostles

The event at Pentecost led to a new expression of God's kingdom, so profound that it had most of the Jews of old completely sold out on the Gospel. It is a common occurrence to miss out on keywords and phrases as one studies the Bible, but keen attention must be paid to each word. This helps to provide a balanced understanding of what the Holy Spirit is trying to teach in that verse. At the start of Acts 3, a word was intentionally used, "Now" in certain translations and "One day" in others. This word or phrase showed a transition, a change, a highlight, or a marker indicating that something different from the norm was about to take place or had taken place, and you are now just witnessing the results of that change. This right here is noteworthy because it shows men who were regular fishermen and tent makers beginning to do things that will leave others in awe of God.

This helps to provide a balanced understanding of what the Holy Spirit is trying to teach in that verse.[20]

The story says that Peter and John, on their way to the temple just as they had done in the past, came upon a man who was lame from birth and was begging for alms at the gate (known as "the Beautiful Gate") of the temple. Although this was not the first time they had seen this man, their encounter with the Holy Spirit would make all their experiences going forward novel and unique. Raising his hands, he sought alms from them, but this time, Peter had better help to offer the lame man – Jesus. Peter clearly stated that he had neither silver nor gold on him, but what he did have, he would give to him, and calling on the name of Jesus, he commands the lame man to rise and walk. On that very day, the lame man received both spiritual and physical healing. There is so much to learn from this singular story that applies to your life today. Often, the wants you so desperately crave can become a thick cloud, blinding you from the all-encompassing power of God. The lame man only had his sights set on the gold he could receive and almost missed the possibility that he could receive both spiritual and physical liberation.

From that "Now" in the first verse of Acts 3, the spread of the Gospel was like a dam breaking loose, taking up all that was on its path. The Bible records that more and more people believed, and multiple signs were given by God through the hands of the Apostles in Acts chapter 5.

> *"The apostles performed many signs and wonders among the people. And all the believers used to meet together in Solomon's Colonnade. No one else dared join the apostles, even though they were highly regarded by the people. Nevertheless, as time went on, more and more men and women believed in the Lord and were added to their number. As a result, people brought the sick into the streets and laid them on beds and mats so that at least Peter's shadow might fall on some of them as he passed by. Crowds gathered also from the towns around Jerusalem, bringing their sick and those tormented by impure spirits, and all of them were healed." Acts 5:12-16 (New International Version).*

The Persecution of the Early Church and Their Challenges

With the rise and spread of the gospel came profound challenges. In Acts 8, you are introduced to the great persecution that was committed against the believers in Jerusalem. They were about to have their fair share of trials and tribulations, just as Jesus had pre-informed them. Right from the time of Jesus, the religious authorities of old, the Pharisees and Sadducees, have posed a strong opposition to the spread of the gospel. Seeing Jesus and his followers as a threat to their authority and leadership, they strongly fought against the advancement of the gospel.

Before the killings came, the opposition started as threats, which led to imprisonment. Before Peter and John were imprisoned, they were warned by the authorities not to preach the gospel, speak, or teach in the name of Jesus, which fueled them to declare Christ even more boldly. With the help of the Holy Spirit in them, they did not cower in fear, and God performed something marvelous for them in the prison. An Angel came that night, released them, and encouraged them to go into the temple and boldly declare the gospel, which astounded the sect of Sadducees. The persecution escalated quickly with the arrest of Stephen, one of the seven chosen for ministry. He was accused of blasphemy and stoned to death, becoming the first martyr of the early Church. Steven, who was stoned for the things he had said, became a trailblazer for future persecutions. Although the arrest of Peter and John after the healing of the lame man is the first record of the opposition the Church faced, it did not get heated until chapters 7 and 8.

The persecution they faced and how they handled it further emphasizes the importance of the apostles waiting for the outpouring of the Holy Spirit. Rather than serve as a damper, the persecution became a catalyst that greatly fueled the spread of the gospel all over Judaea and into parts of Rome.

The persecution and killing of Steven were led by a man called Saul of Tarsus, whom you will later know as Apostle Paul. His transformation from an avid persecutor to an active follower is one worth discussing. Following his leading in the persecution of Steven, Saul began a campaign against anyone who was a follower of Jesus, leaving the believers scrabbling in his wake as he entered into their homes and dragged them out to prison. He was quickly becoming a thorn in the side of the Church, but he had no idea how great the plans God had for him were. On his way to Damascus, after receiving information that there were believers gathered there, he had an encounter that would change his life forever.

While on his way with two other companions, a bright light shines down on them, and he encounters Jesus, which marks his turning point to becoming one of the most revered apostles of the early Church and to date. There is so much to glean from Paul's experience; the drastic change must not have been easy for him. At the start of his work with God, he must have felt lonely because most of the believers had yet to trust him. However, being completely changed, he seized the opportunity to have a relationship with his old crew. Aside from that, moving on from the guilt of the atrocities he committed in his time of ignorance would not have been an easy step.

Even with the conversion of Paul, the challenges continued, but for every challenge, the spread of the gospel soared higher. The opposition came from both the Jewish communities and the Gentile community, which raised internal issues between the Jewish believers and the Gentile converts. Members of the Jewish believers considered the spread of the gospel to the Gentiles wrong. They would not want to associate with them, and some of the apostles, like Peter, also held this belief. It took a vision from God to change his view on that. Peter believed that before redemption would be extended to the Gentile community, they would first have to be converted and become Jews. God revealed to him in a vision that none of the things created by Him can be considered unclean when He, God, had not done so. In the vision, God instructed Peter to kill and eat various beasts, and Peter would not because he considered them unclean. He had the same vision three times before coming to understand what it meant: that God accepted any man who would fear God and work in righteousness and that such man should be accepted by him as well. It was after this that Paul came to him, and Peter was able to accept him in Acts 10.

The lesson here is not to be a judge but to love and receive everything and everyone with the love of God. This newfound understanding would help bridge the gap and aid in the propagation of the gospel all over the world.

It is easy to get lost in the praises of Paul and miss seeing him as a mere human, helped by God. He had many struggles but was able to overcome them all by the power of God at work in him. When you go through life's challenges, you must know that your situation is not unique to you and, most importantly, that the power of God is available to help you get through and come out stronger. Remember, just like Apostle Paul, you are not alone.

The baptizing of Saint Paul.[21]

Moment of Reflection

1. The Day of Pentecost is a pivotal moment in Acts, marked by the outpouring of the Holy Spirit. What are your thoughts on the role of the Holy Spirit in your life today?

2. The book of Acts portrays the early Christian community as sharing everything in common. Reflect on the concept of communal living and generosity. How might this principle be applied around you today?

3. The conversion of Saul (later Paul) is a significant turning point in Acts. Have you ever experienced a transformative moment in your beliefs or values? How did it impact your perspective and actions?

4. The missionary journeys of Paul and other apostles highlight the spread of Christianity to diverse cultures. How do you feel about sharing your newfound faith with others?

5. Acts recount several instances of miraculous healings. If you could perform a healing miracle, what ailment or condition would you choose to address, and why?

6. Reflect on the concept of resilience in the face of persecution, as seen in the lives of early Christians in Acts. How can their experiences inspire your perseverance in challenging circumstances?

7. Peter's vision addresses his questions on the inclusion of Gentiles into the Christian faith. Reflect on moments in your life when you have had to navigate and reconcile differences in beliefs or practices with others.

The story of the early Church shows a union of divine intervention and human determination, which resulted in explosive results. See yourself today through the lens of the early Church and each Apostle talked about in the book of Acts. There are no limitations when you choose to walk and work hand in hand with the Holy Spirit; the results are beyond anything you could ever fathom. The significance of the book of Acts emphasizes the peace, joy, and confidence that Matthew 19:26 brings when it says, "...With God all things are possible!"

Chapter 6: Paul's Letters: Foundations of Christian Doctrine

Paul was referred to by some as the Apostle of Progress; his life was truly progressive in the way in which the world views growth today. Like many, he didn't get it right the first time, but eventually, he did. Paul progressed in ways that have left many and still leave many in awe. Only a few of Jesus' twelve apostles could equal the impact Paul had. This isn't to downplay their roles and efforts in the establishment and advancement of the early Church; they did very important work. However, Paul gave Christians the gift of his epistles on which the early and modern Church foundations are laid. These foundations still hold firm today because of the sacrifices of a man who thought it all as gain to ensure the spread of the good news beyond the borders of Judea.

Who is Paul, and what makes the life of this messenger of grace so profound? You are about to get these questions answered, as this chapter is solely dedicated to his background,

St. Paul."

occupation, service, conversion, trials, missionary journeys, teachings, letters, and ministry in general.

The Early Life of Apostle Paul

Paul, over time, was known as many things: an Apostle, a spiritual pioneer, a critical thinker, Saint Paul, the teacher of the Gentiles, etc. However, before these names existed, he was just *Saul of Tarsus*, a tent maker by trade, a Pharisee by upbringing, and a zealous persecutor of the early Christians.

Saul was recorded as being born in Tarsus, a vibrant city east of Cilicia. Just as with other prominent figures of old, there are discrepancies in the exact location of his birth. Others believed he was born in a town in Galilee called Giscala and later relocated to Tarsus with his parents in the early years of his life. Ascertaining the exact date of his birth has not been possible, but there have been attempts based on gathered information. Since he was referred to as a young man during the persecution of Steven in the Book of Acts and was active in his missionary journeys during the 40s and 50s, it was inferred that he must have been born around the time of Jesus, which is 4 BCE, or a little later. His time of death is also estimated to be around 62-64 CE.

Growing up in Tarsus held a lot of significance in Paul's later years. Tarsus was a prominent town and a province ruled by the Romans, which resulted in its rich cultural diversity. Paul's background as a Roman citizen and a tent maker shaped his ability to adapt to multiple cultures and gave him a sound educational background. This helped him bridge the gap between the Jews and the Gentiles for the gospel's sake during the fulfillment of his ministry. His Jewish education was obtained under the tutelage of Gamaliel, a Pharisee and a highly esteemed Jewish rabbi of his time. He also gained proficiency in other essential areas, like being bilingual and learning the craft of tent making, which provided him with practical and essential skills at that time, as well as financial support during his many missionary journeys.

Paul's Transformation: Adversary to Ally

Paul's conversion from a Pharisee to a major antagonist of the teachings of Pharisaism, a youth from a strongly heathen city to a major critic of all their practices, and a born Hebrew to a strong contender against the Judaic exclusiveness was a miracle.

Paul grew up to attain a high level of strictness, which he used in his approach to the persecution of the early Church. This was due to his educational upbringing by a well-renowned Jewish teacher, which was in perfect accordance with the laws of his fathers. Because of their rigorous adherence to the Mosaic laws, the Jews are known as one of the strictest sects. Still known as Saul of Tarsus in the early chapters of Acts, Paul's devotion to Pharisaism is seen in his zeal towards the persecution of the early Church. He fervently opposed what he considered to be a deviation from Judaism. In the eighth and ninth chapters, it was revealed how far he was willing to go to uphold his beliefs. In Acts 8:1-3 and Acts 9:1-2, Paul's role was significant in the punishment given to all who chose to follow Jesus, consenting at one point to the stoning of Stephen, the very first Christian martyr. In his own words, as you would later read in 1 Timothy 1:13, he describes himself at this time of his life as a persecutor, blasphemer, and insolent man. However, all these versions of him were about to change for the better.

In 1 Timothy 1:13, he describes himself at this time of his life as a persecutor, blasphemer, and insolent man.[23]

His victory in conquering and persecuting the Church fueled his ambitions. It raised his stakes when he persecuted Christians from other towns and cities. This pushed him to travel down to Damascus from Jerusalem in the hope of finding followers of Christ there. It was on this very journey that his conversion took place; he was said to be "arrested by God." As Saul journeyed with his companions, having received a letter from the High priest permitting him to persecute the Christians of the Damascus synagogue, he experienced the most transformative moment of his life. During the encounter, a bright light shone down from heaven upon him, and he heard a voice, as seen in Acts 9:4-6

> "And he fell to the earth, and heard a voice saying unto him, 'Saul, Saul, why persecutest thou me?' And he said, 'Who art thou, Lord?' And the Lord said, 'I am Jesus whom thou persecutest: it is hard for thee to kick against the pricks.' And he, trembling and astonished, said, 'Lord, what wilt thou have me to do?' And the Lord said unto him, 'Arise, and go into the city, and it shall be told thee what thou must do.'"

The intensity of the encounter blinded him, and he was supported for the rest of the journey to Damascus. While he was there, he remained blind for three days, and he neither ate nor drank. In those moments, God was instructing one of his servants, Ananias, to go to Paul and help him restore his sight, and Ananias, knowing Paul's reputation, was hesitant. Nonetheless, he went in full obedience to God's instructions. Coming into Paul's house, he healed, baptized, and filled him with the Holy Spirit, which marked his birthing into the Christian faith. Following his conversion, Paul didn't delay; he was immediately seen declaring Jesus as Christ in the synagogue. Many found it hard to believe that the leading man in the persecution of the Church, who had come down to Damascus for that very reason, was now advocating for the very cause he had fought against.

Although many were astonished, others, like the Jewish leaders, were not pleased and sought to kill him. Being aware of the threat to his life, he escaped in a basket through an opening in the city wall with the help of the disciples present. From then on, he stepped into a new chapter in his life, one completely devoted to the spread of the gospel, and with a change in his name from Saul to Paul. This new phase in Paul's life stands as a stark contrast to the pre-transformed Saul, which shows the profound impact of his encounter with the risen Christ on the road to Damascus. This transition from persecutor to Apostle highlights the transformative power of Grace and redemption in Paul's journey.

Paul's Epistles

In the many epistles written by the Apostle Paul, you can perceive his literary prowess. However, the ability to take down his epistles was less attributed to his expertise in writing and more to the Holy Spirit's divine work through him. Paul's Letters, being foundational to the New Testament, shaped Christian theology.

Here is a detailed overview of these letters and their purpose;

Romans: Unveiling the Foundations of Faith

The Book of Romans was originally written for the Christian Church in Rome and, by extension, also for modern Christians today. Outside its powerful message, its clear, comprehensible, concise, and systemic style of presenting the Christian doctrine makes it a quick favorite of young or new Christians. At the beginning of a new Christian's Bible study, Romans always make it on the list of first reads.

The Apostle Paul wrote the Epistle to the Romans to address several key theological and pastoral concerns within the Christian community in Rome. He addressed topics ranging from the believers' justification by faith and the righteousness of God to the world's need for salvation. The theological richness that Romans possess makes it a cornerstone of the Christian doctrine. At the time Apostle Paul wrote this Letter to the Roman Church, the Christian community in Rome consisted of both Jews and Gentiles. It is not news that there was discrimination towards the Gentiles by the Jewish Christians. In his letter, he emphasized the importance of unity and mutual understanding among them while highlighting their shared salvation through faith in Christ Jesus in Romans 15:5-7. It is very easy for strife to come in between relationships when you are not being watchful, even for the most minute reasons. It could be between your spouse, sibling, friend, child, or co-worker. etc., but you are encouraged by Paul always to remember that you are to receive each person just the same way Christ received you.

1st and 2nd Corinthians: Wisdom and Guidance for the Church

Similar to Romans' advocacy for unity and oneness, the books of Corinthians addressed the Church in Corinth, a major city in Greece. It is one of the key books in the New Testament that focuses on a single union within God's body. Corinth, being a city that served as the center of Greek culture, was a commercial city teeming with people from all around the world, meaning this was reflected in the total population of the Church. The diverse nature of the Church meant disagreements were almost inevitable, and love and harmony became the second most discussed topic after immorality for the Corinth Christians.

The subject of morality was also a major one for the Corinthian Church, and they struggled greatly with it. Raised in the heart of Greece with its pagan ways, where sexual rites are common occurrences at every feast and ceremony, and words like chastity and monogamy were novel, these new Christians found it difficult to uphold morality. So, Apostle Paul saw the need to put more effort into addressing it. Besides Paul's address of these two topics, he also talked about other things, such as the misuse of spiritual gifts. He gave guidance on such topics as marriage and the Lord's supper in the first part of Corinthians. The second part of this book is concerned with Paul's defense of his apostleship, discussing what the true nature of a Christian ministry should look like and encouraging followers to live in light of the new covenant. Generally, a central theme for both books is an address on the balance of grace and discipline among a diverse Christian community.

Galatians: Freedom in Christ's Grace

Apostle Paul leads the Galatian Church through a series of teachings and exhortations in his letter to them. Addressed to them at Galatia, his letter was centered on the theme of Grace as he vehemently opposed any form of legalistic teaching making its way into their Church. In this letter, he aimed to show them their complete sufficiency of faith in Christ for their Salvation, clearing them of any form of doubt that they needed the law, that is, the Jewish tenets, to guarantee their justification in Christ.

Key themes in Galatians are the justification of faith, freedom in Christ, and crucifixion with Christ. In Galatians 6:14, Paul informs the Church of Galatia, "But far be it from me to boast except in the cross of our Lord Jesus Christ, by which the world has been crucified to me, and I to the world." Here, he talks to them about being identified in Christ's death and resurrection and how this union with Christ transforms the Christian life. Another profound scripture on the topic of justification of faith is Galatians 2:16:

"Yet we know that a person is not justified by works of the law but through faith in Jesus Christ, so we also have believed in Christ Jesus, to be justified by faith in Christ and not by works of the law, because by works of the law, no one will be justified."

This scripture teaches you that justification can only come through one source, which is faith in Christ; any other attempt by one's effort will prove futile. Trying to earn salvation on your terms and by your effort shows you are undermining the finished work of Christ. This is said while not undermining the place of spiritual discipline.

Ephesians: The Unity of the Body in Christ

While on his third missionary journey, Apostle Paul was in the City of Ephesus for more than two years, where he ministered to the people there. Being a city that housed the Greek goddess Artemi's temple, many opposed his ministry for different reasons. Still, many were also converted to the faith. After he left, he was imprisoned for the first time, and it is believed that it was there that he wrote the Ephesians Epistle along with other letters to the Philippians, Colossians, and Philemon. The book of Ephesians took on a more formal approach. Whether because of its importance or his lesser acquaintance with the Church in Ephesus remains unknown.

In this letter, Paul talks about topics that are at the very core of a Christian's belief in both faith and practice. He addressed topics on the mystery of God's will, unity in Christ, and spiritual warfare. Within the first three chapters of the letter, Paul talks about how God, through the gift of Grace in Jesus Christ's death and resurrection, created a special and holy community. In this community, He has specially chosen individuals whom He has adopted as His sons and daughters through Christ's accomplishments. Regardless of being a Jew or a Gentile, everyone who becomes a partaker of this grace was once dead spiritually because of their wrongdoings but has now been brought into life through the deeds of Christ alone.

While not attempting to address just a particular problem in their morals or theology, his focus was on avoiding future problems by getting the followers of the Ephesian Church to grow in their faith and become mature Christians. After elaborating on these profound theological truths in the first half of the book, Paul straightforwardly expressed his expectation: he envisioned that this community of Christians would embody its heavenly calling. So, by seeking to divide the letter into segments in his address, although not intentionally, the first part shows you the truth, and by applying the truth, the lifestyle talked about in the second part becomes possible to fulfill. Scriptural verses like Ephesians 1:9-10, Ephesians 4, Ephesians 6, etc., address these topics directly to give you a better understanding.

Philippians: Joy in Unity and Christ-likeness

The book of Philippians is one of the books in the New Testament, and it scores as a great hit among today's Christians due to its great and easily relatable verses. All books of the Bible have their fair share of popular verses, but Philippians have a host of them. A verse like Philippians 1:6, which says, *"He who began a good work in you will carry it on to completion until the day of Christ."* conveys hope beautifully; it serves as a reassurance when you feel overwhelmed or on the verge of giving up.

Another one of such great verses that stir up faith within you is Philippians 4:13, which says, *"I can do all things through him who strengthens me."* This verse gives you the boldness and confidence to go through the hardest of challenges, the confidence not in your ability but in the excellent power of God. A third one is, *"For me to live is Christ and to die is gain."* as seen in Philippians 1:21. This statement by Paul shows you the insignificance of this world without the purpose of fulfilling Christ and the reward of a better life to come after this world.

However, originally written to the Church in Philippi while Paul was in prison, these verses are loved and appreciated by the Church and were written to address key themes like joy in all circumstances, unity and humility, pressing toward Christlikeness, and the surpassing worth of knowing Christ. He radiates a theme of joy amidst challenging circumstances. When in prison, he expresses gratitude for the Church's partnership in the gospel and shares profound insights on Christian living.

Colossians: Embracing the Fullness of Christ's Supremacy

The Epistle to the Colossians, likely written by Paul during his imprisonment in Rome (around AD 60-62), unveils the profound teachings regarding the supremacy of Christ. This letter, addressed to the Church in Colossae, is a powerful exposition on the all-sufficiency of Christ in matters of faith and Salvation. The Colossae church was believed to have been established during his third missionary journey by one of his converts, a Colossian visiting Ephesus, Epaphras. In response to the good news he had heard from Paul, he returned to his city to share it with them. This scenario was like the story of the Samaritan woman who came in contact with Jesus in John 4:5-30 and yielded the same result.

This scenario was like the story of the Samaritan woman who came in contact with Jesus in John 4:5-30 and yielded the same result.[24]

The first reaction after receiving the gospel with joy is always to share it. As a Christian, proof of the word of God being implanted in your heart is in your desire and zeal to share it with others. Although Paul never had the opportunity to visit the Colossian Church, through his interface with Epaphras, he is made aware of the struggles faced in the Church, and he wasted no time in addressing them head-on. He wrote the Colossian Epistle after finding out that the supremacy of Christ's rule as the head of the Church and as the son of God was being demeaned by some false teachers.

The Church at Colossae was under attack from false teachers who were denigrating the deity of Jesus; they were teaching that He was not actually God. Paul addressed these issues by emphasizing the preeminence of Christ in creation, redemption, and the reconciliation of all things, urging Christians to acknowledge and embrace His comprehensive supremacy, as you would see in, Colossians 1:15-20, *"He is the image of the invisible God, the firstborn of all creation... For in him all the fullness of God was pleased to dwell."*

He also discussed other subjects, like finding complete fullness in God and living life totally in Him. He warned them not to consider other notions like deceptive philosophies and human traditions and to embrace virtues like compassion, kindness, humility, patience, and gentleness in Christ.

1st and 2nd Thessalonians: Embracing Hope, Holy Living, and End-Times Expectation

The letters to the Thessalonians, probably written by Paul in the early 50s AD, focused on the anticipation of Christ's return, the importance of living a holy life, and guides what to expect in the end times. However, intended for the Christians at Thessalonica, these epistles offer encouragement, practical advice, and insights into what to expect in the future. Its core message is on the anticipation and hope a Christian should have concerning Christ's second coming. He addresses their concerns when they inquire about the fate of a departed Christian by teaching them in depth the events that surround Christ's second coming and practical Holy Christian living, a quiet life, excelling in love, and working diligently.

A scripture that can quickly make it onto your list of favorites is 1 Thessalonians 5:16-18. Paul states, "Rejoice always, pray without ceasing, give thanks in all circumstances; for this is the will of God in Christ Jesus for you." It is a soothing and encouraging charge, one that can bring about peace and calm when you hold on to it wholeheartedly.

Other Epistles: Navigating the Pauline Wisdom and Pastoral Counsel

The remaining book collection of Pauline Epistles, comprising Timothy, Titus, Philemon, and Hebrews, adds the extra finesse needed by Christians for a well-grounded understanding of the way of life for the new era of Christianity. Some of these letters may not have been written by Paul directly, but they are in line with his teachings. They address multiple themes, from topics on leadership and Christian conduct to your relationship with God and Christ's supremacy. Although some of these subjects have been touched on in the previous books, these last epistles lay a much-needed emphasis on them again for your sake. For example, the book of Hebrews dedicates ample chapters to talking about the supremacy of Christ, providing crucial insights into the topic of the new covenant and the significance of faith.

Moments of Reflection

1. Is there a change in your view of salvation based on Apostle Paul's teaching of justification by faith?

2. How can you contribute to fostering unity within your local Christian community?

3. Reflect on Paul's metaphor of the body. How does it shape your view of diversity within the Church?

4. What spiritual gifts do you believe God has given you, and how can you use them to serve others?

5. How does Paul's description of love in Corinthians 13 inspire your relationships with others?

6. Reflect on a time when you experienced comfort from God. How dis it impact your faith?

7. In which areas of your life do you need to pursue reconciliation, following Paul's teachings?

8. How does recognizing the supremacy of Christ influence your perspective on life's challenges?

9. Reflecting on your identity in Christ, how does it shape your self-worth and purpose?

10. In challenging circumstances, how can you maintain a spirit of joy, as encouraged by Paul?

11. Reflect on the role of gratitude in your life and its connection to joy.

In what way can you cultivate humility in your interactions with others? How does Paul's model of servant leadership challenge your common perceptions of leadership?

The life of the Apostle Paul stands as a testament to the transformative power of God's grace. His journey from a zealous persecutor to a devoted follower of Christ reflects the profound impact of encountering Jesus Christ. Paul's epistles, filled with theological depth and practical wisdom, continue to guide and inspire Christians today. As you navigate the pages of his letters, you will find a road map for living out the Christian faith with authenticity, love, and a steadfast hope in the promises of Christ. The enduring legacy of Paul extends beyond the 1st-century churches, resonating with believers of every era, inviting them to embrace the grace that transforms lives and to walk in the light of Christ's redemptive love.

Chapter 7: Revelations

Many are curious about the future and will do anything to have a glimpse of what it holds. This desire is not exactly wrong, as it's a part of a human being's general make-up. God doesn't want you to be ignorant about the things He wants you to do, and if you find yourself not in God's plan, it's because you haven't aligned completely with Him. This can be verified all through the Bible, where you see God reveal His will and plans to His servants who are in total service to Him. Some of these things are yet to happen, but He made them open and public to anyone who cares or is interested in knowing what will happen in the future. In books like Daniel, Ezekiel,

God reveals his plans in the book of Revelation.[25]

Isaiah, Joel, Zechariah, and the major one dedicated to this cause, Revelation, you will see prophecies made about what is to come at the end of the world and the fate of the followers of Christ.

God has revealed His plans to His faithful servants so that they may share them with His children. Although the relevance or significance of this book is not limited to just that, neither is it primarily about the future. There is so much more that can be harnessed from the book of Revelation, and an understanding of this will help you grow and improve your knowledge of God and His will for you.

Revelation Introduced

The book of Revelation is derived from the Greek word "Apokalypsis," which means "Unveiling" or "Revelation." Unlike the Old Testament, the Book of Revelation is the only apocalyptic book in the New Testament. This book is one of the most challenging for Christians due to the vivid imagery and symbolism contained in it. Many would rather read any other book of the Bible than Revelation. Having an understanding of this book through an overview will help you see the weight of the message contained in it and build your interest in grasping every lesson you can get by reading the entire book. A greater challenge than its comprehension is its application. You have to be willing to make key adjustments in the areas pointed out by the writer. However, it is worth noting that with this great challenge comes great blessings.

In the past, the book of Revelation was generally accepted to be under the authorship of the great Apostle John, who also wrote the books the Gospel of John and 1st, 2nd, and 3rd John, meaning he wasn't new to penning down experiences and sharing his knowledge and walk with God in writing. It is deduced that his role as an apostle of the early Church, with a lot of influence, was the reason why he did not see the need to add a title, as the people to whom he wrote were well acquainted with him, and his name alone was enough introduction. These and more were the basis by which earlier scholars accepted Apostle John, popularly known as "John the Beloved," as the author of this book.

In recent times, there has been a great variation in thoughts and ideas towards the authorship of the book of Revelation. Modern-day scholars and theologians state that just a name alone given within this book is not enough to certify that John the Beloved actually wrote it, and all that is known of the author is that he was a Christian prophet. They claim it could have been any John who ministered back then. They also claim there's a difference in the writing styles used in the Gospel of John and the other books (1st, 2nd, and 3rd Books of John) and that of the book of Revelation. Other scholars who believed that John the Beloved wrote Revelation have rebuffed this argument, stating that the genres of both books are different, and this can affect the writing style used. They also claim that anyone in the state he was when the book was written, on the Aegean Island of Patmos, located off the west coast of Asia Minor, would write differently and that he also lacked the advanced scholarly items used for writing as of that time and could not possibly have had access to them on that island.

Modern scholars still stand firmly on their beliefs that it could be any John – and the evidence provided for Apostle John's case is not solid enough to make a definite decision that he authored this book. With this understanding, they have resolved to always refer to the Author of Revelation as simply "John of Patmos" or "John the Elder" to achieve a common ground.

Historical Context

Revelation, written in 96 CE, was a time in John's life when the Romans ruled over large parts of major continents like Africa, Europe, and Asia, where the churches John was addressing were situated. This very factor had a major significance in John's address. At a time when the majority of Asians were apathetic towards Christian doctrines, some remained steadfast in the apostles' doctrine. This did not go well with the then Roman Emperor, Nero, who commanded the execution of all Christians, and this decree was likely to be emulated by the Emperor, Domitian, who was leaning towards the persecution of the Church as well, as they would

Emperor Nero commanded the execution of all Christians.[96]

not bow and worship him like all others. This was a highly crucial time for the Christians, as the advocation for Emperor worship was on the rise. It is also worth noting that this very factor was the reason John was on the Island of Patmos. He was exiled there for preaching the gospel and declaring Jesus as Lord.

The Apocalyptic Genre of Revelation

The book of Revelation adopted a unique writing style called an apocalyptic genre, commonly found within Jewish and Christian texts. Similar to prophecy, apocalyptic literature communicates revelations from visions and dreams. It is often a combination of elements of reality and fantasy. Books like Daniel also share similar themes and literary devices. Deciphering the core message was likely more effortless for the initial recipients at that time than for today's readers who are unfamiliar with this literary style. Individuals of that era were used to this writing style because it was prevalent. As a modern reader, you will have to adopt an "ancient eyes" perspective, which involves understanding the literary conventions of that time and the historical events that prompted the utilization of such a distinctive style. That is, the only way to have a rich understanding of an apocalyptic book is to view it through a lens that reflects the mindset of its original audience.

The Letters to the Seven Churches: Unveiling Divine Insights

In the book of Revelation, letters were addressed to the seven churches, and each letter combines symbolic language with vivid imagery to provide timeless significance and relevance in today's world. This book, although written by John, was written in full obedience to Jesus Christ's instructions. He was instructed to write to the seven Asian churches, namely, Ephesus, Smyrna, Pergamum, Thyatira, Sardis, Philadelphia, and Laodicea, to warn and encourage them as they underwent different struggles, both internal problems, like laxity & morality, and external challenges, such as persecution and execution from the Roman empire. Following the introduction and instructions, we see John's address to these seven churches in the 2nd and 3rd chapters. Each Church receives a message with its letter that addresses their unique struggles and how to make adjustments.

At the start of the first vision in Revelation 1:20, John sees seven candlesticks, like that seen by Zechariah in Zechariah 4:2. The candles represent the seven churches he would be addressing. A candlestick is a good depiction of the Church, which is meant to represent the light in this dark world and shows its role in helping others receive the light. The candlestick, where seven stars were said to represent the Angels, was believed to be the church leaders back then. For all seven churches, the template was the same when writing their letters, but the content differed. It always begins by commending the Church, followed by words of encouragement, then reproof, and ends with counsel on how to return from their errors, and finally, a promise of hope on what they stand to gain by being faithful. The message to the Church wasn't just to the Church alone, but to all those struggling to stand firm on their choice in service to God.

The Loveless Church: Letter to the Church in Ephesus

The Ephesian Church is a story of returning to one's first love. In the letter, Jesus urges them to remember, repent, and then return. This is a complete process, one that is also expected of every Christian today. The letter to the Church in Ephesus was written in the time of the early Church when the apostles were still alive, and the city was in its prime. Being a city with a vibrant metropolis made it the center for trade and commerce and a hub for Greek spiritual activity, as it was a city dedicated to the Greek goddess Artemis.

John began the letter to the Ephesus with praises for their tireless zeal and unrelenting dedication to the growth and spread of the gospel. It is worth noting that Jesus, in the vision to John, didn't just begin with reproof; he commended their good work. This shows that total service to God isn't just commendable; it's worth emulating. Serving God and watching Him change the lives of others through you is deeply satisfying. Their refusal and distaste of the teachings and actions of some groups back then – ones that didn't mind engaging in immoral acts as long as it hurt no one – was another plus for the Ephesian Church (and one for which they were commended). This group, called the "Nicolaitans" didn't think it necessary to put a stop to the desires of the flesh. They thought it all alright to act as they liked, engaging in the pleasures of the flesh, while they still claimed to be in service to God. They tried to share this opinion with the rest of the body of the Church, but the Ephesians would not cave in. However, they got caught up in their desire to serve God, and they lost sight of their hearts until they were no longer driven by their love for Jesus.

This raises the question, how does one stay busy for Jesus without loving him? Well, you saw it with the Church in Ephesus. The Bible doesn't say what their motivation was; there could have been a host of reasons, but one possibility is religiosity, meaning being busy just for the sake of it. This goes to show that it's possible to not love God and serve in His house, but it is impossible to love God and not serve in His house. This is a crucial revaluation that all Christians should take regularly. Ask yourself, "Is my heart right with God? Do I do the things I do out of love for Him or because of religion?" For the Ephesians, their actions were not the problem; Jesus was more focused on their motivation. What fueled the things they did?

The Ephesus church had grown cold in heart, and their service to Him had become ritualistic. Here, Jesus provides counsel on what to do. He says that they should remember what it was like when they had just found Him and how vibrant, fiery, and alive their hearts were for Him, and then urges them to repent. It is one thing to remember and realize your faults and wrongdoings, but it is a completely different thing to be willing to change and chart a new course for yourself, regardless of how far gone you are. Aside from the reproof and counsel, He also lets them know that there would always be a repercussion for their actions and what would happen if they were not quick to change. He, however, did not leave them trembling at the thought of the consequences of their actions but offered them hope as well, via a promise. He assured them there was a tree of life of which they would eat and an eternal paradise awaiting them; this would keep them in high spirits as they worked towards change.

A beautiful thing worth noting about God's method is that after He highlights the problem to you patiently, He doesn't leave you alone to figure out how to go about it. He takes further steps by explaining its consequences and how they can greatly affect you and then leaves you to make an informed decision without pressure because He has given us the ability of free will.

The Persecuted Church: Letter to the Church in Smyrna

The Church in Smyrna, also called the suffering church, is a perfect example of beauty from ashes. When faced with the toughest of persecutions, rather than being crushed by it, it served as a stepping stone for them to ride upon and show forth the glory of God. This letter to Smyrna was one of comfort and assurance to those who were in troubling times. Jesus began by saying to them, "I know." This was a reassurance for them that they were not alone, that He saw their struggles, and that in due time, He would bring them out stronger and better. For the Church in Smyrna, unlike the others, there was no reproof; that wasn't what they needed; rather, the words spoken to them at that time were words of encouragement.

To better understand the state this Church was in, it's believed that the leader presiding over the Church was a man called Polycarp, who in the height of Roman worship, was burned at the stake because he refused to pledge allegiance to the Roman Emperor and swear his loyalty by offering incense. It didn't stop there; Emperors like Marcus Aurelius, Vespasian, and Domitian, in their relentless pursuit, would have them placed in extremely shabby prisons, dragged into the arenas in rags, burned, killed and fed to the wild beasts of the field. Jesus then comforts them by encouraging them to be faithful and assures them of His knowledge of their situation and His presence with them. Although they faced intense persecution, this Church did not give in to the ways of the Romans. They thought it worthwhile to endure the pain and hardship in the name of Jesus Christ, hoping to obtain an incorruptible crown in the end. A thought-provoking conclusion is that the Church with the strongest persecutions turns out to be the purest. Holding fast to God's word in the face of adversity is the best approach to sailing through.

The Compromising Church: Letter to the Church in Pergamos

Unlike the Ephesian Church, the Church in Pergamos gave ears to the ways of the Nicolaitans, and they began to drift away from the word of God and found themselves giving in to the ways of their environment. They went after wealth and luxury at the expense of their work with God. It wasn't that they didn't love God; they were made to believe that they could love God and love their present world, too, and no one has to suffer. However, Jesus came very direct in His message of repentance to them. He gave them the same counsel as Ephesus: repent, return, and change.

The Corrupt Church: Letter to the Church in Thyatira

Just as in His message to the loveless Church, Jesus began with commendations for their efforts in getting better, acknowledging their deeds, love, faith, service, and perseverance. After this, Jesus dives right into the reproof; although there was no mention of the Nicolaitans, the Thyatira church was said to engage in their approved practices, which the Christian faith disapproves. Beyond being a place of trade, Thyatira was also a place of war, and this made it difficult for the people to get by. The only known way of survival for them was being a part of the trade guild, which was of huge importance to civic society at that time. The guilds were known to eat the meals offered to idols and engage in other idolatrous acts. This became a problem for the Christians. Jesus encourages them to let go of their idolatrous ways and turn to Him. He lets them know the consequences of not listening to Him. Also, He tells them about the promise made to those who heed His words; to those who overcome, He would give authority over the nations and many more things.

The Dead Church: Letter to the Church in Sardis

The letter written to this Church was written at a time when there was a deep fallout of Christians in the early Church, but even with this, there remained those who upheld the light of the gospel. The Sardinian Church was a church with a false show of righteousness; they made promises without fulfillment, and their outward display of strength showed careless confidence and want in their watchfulness. The message to the Church in Sardis was not really one of condemnation but more of disapproval. They were called hypocrites who made a show of a burning passion for the things of God but were actually dead inside. Jesus talks about not finding their works perfect, meaning they made an effort to work, but that was only to put up a front that they still had everything put together. Jesus would rather they acknowledge they have lost their way, retrace their steps, go back, and start again than act like they are still on the right track.

The Sardis church fell at a time when the Church seemed to be living in its past glory; they had come to a halt and were stalling but refused to acknowledge and address the problem. They had grown content in resting on their past victor's laurels.

The Faithful Church: Letter to the Church in Philadelphia

The city of Philadelphia was a major Grecian town because its main purpose was to spread and promote the unity of customs, spirits, and loyalty for the sake of the empire. It was very successful in its pursuit of the empire. This means there was a strong practice of the Grecian way in Philadelphia, but regardless, the Church remained faithful. Jesus commends them greatly when He said they possessed little strength but did a lot and didn't give in at any moment to the ways and systems of their present society. There were no reproofs for this Church, but he made many heartwarming promises. He promised them an open door, which no man would ever be able to close, and a show of His power over those who opposed them.

The letter to the Church of Philadelphia challenges today's Christians. Jesus mentioned that with what little strength they had, they persevered, meaning you're never to say you're without help or strength. You should also trust in the depth of God's love to help you in every circumstance.

The Lukewarm Church: Letter to the Church in Laodiceans

As you would see in your study of this Church, they seemed to be the worst of the bunch. There were no commendations given to them by Jesus. He rather dived right into their problems and His reproof of their attitude. He began again with the same phrase used in His address to the other churches, "I know." This shows that there truly is nothing that can be hidden from the sight of God; He sees right into the deepest thoughts of your heart. This Church was in a worse state because it was hard to find them anywhere, just as Jesus described them to be neither cold nor hot. This statement meant they did not openly accept Jesus, nor did they openly reject Him, and made the house of God seem like a social club where they gathered to have fun.

For this reason, Jesus said He would spit them out of His mouth. Following the reproof, Jesus still acknowledged them as the ones He loves, urging them to repent. This shows just how much God loves His Children, that even in their filth, His love still shines through, calling them out into His light.

The letter to the seven churches, although written to actual locations in the 1st century, carries a great spiritual significance today. It addresses the state of hearts that exists within the Church. When you examine yourself thoroughly and with all honesty, you will find areas of your life aligning with one or more of the cases of the churches in Asia Minor. So, it's advised that you deeply study these letters, the reproofs, corrections, and counsels to shape your life better.

The Other Visions

In the Book of Revelation, the shift from the letters to the seven churches reveals a vivid picture of events and symbols: seven seals being opened, seven trumpets sounding, and seven bowls pouring out God's wrath. This apocalyptic tale has sparked various interpretations, with Christians and scholars grappling over what these visions truly mean. One widely accepted view suggests that these symbols represent a spiritual struggle between good and evil. The seven seals, trumpets, and bowls are seen as metaphors for an ongoing battle throughout history — a clash between the forces of goodness and malevolence. This perspective argues that these visions depict the enduring fight between God's plan for salvation and disruptive forces trying to thwart it. Key figures, like the Antichrist and the two witnesses, are often seen as symbolic representations rather than literal individuals.

On the flip side, some interpret these visions more literally, proposing specific historical and future events. The seals, trumpets, and bowls are thought to be concrete predictions of wars, natural disasters, and divine judgments in a specific chronological order. This perspective views the imagery as a kind of road map for understanding God's divine plan as it unfolds over time. The identity of the Antichrist and the interpretation of the final battle between good and evil becomes a central point of contention. Some argue that these are symbolic representations of societal and spiritual conflicts.

In contrast, others insist on a more straightforward reading, pointing to specific historical figures or future individuals embodying these roles. This disagreement sparks heated debates over the timing and nature of these apocalyptic events. The role

The seven seals, trumpets, and bowls are seen as metaphors for an ongoing battle throughout history — a clash between the forces of goodness and malevolence.[27]

of the two witnesses is another puzzle, with interpretations ranging from symbolic representations of God's faithful messengers to claims of their literal presence during a future period of tribulation. This diversity in perspectives reflects the complexity of Revelation's imagery and the challenge of making sense of symbolic language in connection with historical or future occurrences.

Debates also arose over the timeline of these events. Some believe in a futurist interpretation, suggesting that most of Revelation's prophecies are to unfold in a specific end-time scenario. Others take a historicist perspective, connecting the visions to events throughout history. Meanwhile, preterists argue that many of the prophecies were fulfilled in the early centuries of the Christian era. In the unfolding narrative of Revelation, different angles of interpretation come together, creating a complex and intricate understanding of these apocalyptic visions. The challenge lies in navigating the tension between symbolic and literal readings, accepting diverse perspectives while seeking to grasp the underlying messages that transcend time and cultural contexts. As Christians and scholars continue exploring Revelation, the rich and varied nature of its imagery ensures that debates over its meaning will persist, offering a fertile ground for theological exploration and reflection.

Moments of Reflection

1. Explore the historical tidbits shared about early Christian communities. How might understanding the context enhance your appreciation of Revelation's messages?

2. What are your thoughts on the messages of hope and salvation woven throughout the narrative, and how do these themes resonate with your spiritual journey?

3. How has your perspective on the book evolved, and what questions or mysteries still linger in your mind?

4. Think about the relevance of Revelation's messages in today's world. How might its themes of justice, redemption, and divine intervention speak to issues and challenges today?

5. Consider the role of faith and perseverance in the face of adversity, as depicted in Revelation within the Church in Smyrna. How do you draw strength from these themes in your own life?

6. Ponder the idea of Revelation as both a warning and a comfort. How do you balance the urgency of its message with the assurance of God's ultimate victory?

Beyond the disagreements that arise from trying to understand this book, for the Christian, there is so much knowledge and insight to be drawn from its pages. Rather than trying to follow the debates, focus more on the light within its pages that offers you a chance at a better Christian journey. The exploration of the book of Revelation is not a one-time deal; its message endures, meaning a revisit often, is necessary. You should employ continuous study and reflection on its lessons.

Chapter 8: Old Testament Prophets: Voices of Warning and Hope

The prophets within the books of the Old Testament can be pictured as messengers chosen by God to communicate directly with Him. Their role in the stories of God's chosen people is profound, offering you a window into a world of guidance, warnings, and hope in diverse situations. They can also be envisioned as ancient heroes, standing up for what's right in a world filled with challenges. As you look into the Bible, there's hardly a key event of that time not tied to their influence.

The prophets within the books of the Old Testament can be pictured as messengers chosen by God to communicate directly with Him.[28]

Explore the stories of these messengers, the crucial messages they conveyed to the people of ancient Israel, and the impact they had, not only in their time but in the lasting relevance of their teachings today. As you navigate the intricate nature of their experiences, consider how their words and messages can serve as beacons of insight in your own life.

A Prophet and His Role

A prophet is someone who interacts with God on behalf of His people. Prophets in the Old Testament were figures who spoke on behalf of God, warning the Israelites about their sins and calling them to repentance; they played an integral role in communicating God's will and purpose during a time of political crises. Their messages were not always the same or conveyed in the same manner; some messages can be more dramatic than others. Certain prophets, like Zechariah and Ezekiel, were able to see elaborate visions. Some played the roles of a mediator or a judge. In contrast, others, like Malachi and Torah, dedicated their lives to working to mend the people's relationship with God, constantly urging them to remember the allegiance they made with the God of Israel and the Torah, which means the Law. Only those who fell under these rules are regarded as prophets.

In some cases in the Old Testament, certain persons spoke or wrote prophetic statements. Still, these people are not considered prophets of the Old Testament. Such a person would be Saul, the first king of Israel, in 1 Samuel 10:9-12, who, under the influence of God's Spirit, prophesied, although what he prophesied about was not recorded in the Bible. However, he prophesied, but the role he played in the Story of Israel is not a prophetic one as he was not called to be a prophet. For this reason, the Bible does not count him as a prophet.

The Major Prophets

The major prophets were significant figures who played pivotal roles during a tumultuous time in Israel's history. They proclaimed a consistent message, warning God's people about the consequences of disobedience while offering a future hope of restoration. Their words provided a sobering reminder for all generations of the importance of staying faithful to God's covenant. At the same time, they broadcast God's steadfast love and promise of new life on the other side of judgment. The fact that you get to study these ancient prophets' messages shows their timeless relevance.

Isaiah: The Messianic Prophet

Isaiah, a key prophet among the Israelites, emerged as a learned voice expressing crucial topics in the divine plan of God. He was an advocate for righteousness, truth, and unwavering faith in God in his teachings, which was during the time of Israel's turbulent monarchy. His book, which is named after him, Isaiah, now stands as the epitome of prophetic writing. The prophet's mention of the "Suffering Servant" evidently teaches about Christ's role as the servant and the agonies that will come with His mission. Isaiah goes beyond writing about events; he charged against moral downfall and worship of idols and called for repentance and heeding to the Word of God. Despite these warnings, he still gives out flickers of hope, persuasively telling people that the path of goodness is the way out to God. The prophetic visions by Isaiah rose above the social, political, and religious context of his time to explore the universal themes of justice, mercy, and the transcendent nature of the divine-human relationship.

His role as one of the prophets of the Old Testament remained influential even in the New Testament, which confirmed the fulfillment of his prophecies on Jesus Christ. Holy writers and Apostles specifically drew parallels with Isaiah's thoughts, which reaffirms his critical place in our comprehension of the messianic role of Jesus Christ.

Jeremiah: The Weeping Prophet

Jeremiah, a towering major prophet, becomes a strong voice in the Old Testament, profoundly shaping the divine narrative. The importance of his work is manifested far above the scope of his book in his principle to get the message that carries elements of warning, lamentation, and hope across. In Israel's history, Jeremiah's prophetic ministry unfolded amid political crises, invasion, and exile. As Jerusalem faced tragic exile, Jeremiah perceived its gravity, recognizing the city's portrayal of profound suffering.

The book of Jeremiah has diverse themes, such as favor and punishment from the Lord, repentance, and the restoration of people from captivity. It explains how the world is not a place where individuals can do whatever they want, the reality of judgment, and a hope of revival. Jeremiah's prophecies were more symbolic, like when he used a potter's clay to illustrate how humans were predominantly under the control of the Almighty. Towards the end, loyal scribes received a critical message introducing the concept of a new covenant and a promising hope amid judgment chaos. Along with this covenant, God mentioned a time when His law would be engraved on hearts, symbolizing a definitive change from the heart.

Jeremiah ("the weeping prophet") has demonstrated his compassion for his people by preaching the hard message while also bearing personal sufferings. He was quite ready to bear the losses for the sake of the sacredness of his calling. Jeremiah's implication serves as a timeless reminder of moral and spiritual decay. The battles he fought, the tears he shed, and the hopes he clung to should remind you of the difficulties faced at different times in your life. Jeremiah transcends his time in the pages of the Old Testament and becomes a beacon symbolizing eternal truth. His poems are filled with discoveries about faith and reveal his thoughts about God, reflecting human life.

Ezekiel: The Visionary Prophet

Ezekiel, one of the major prophets in the Old Testament, is a tremendously striking and assertive persona that no one can ignore. Considering the length of his book, Ezekiel, as the messenger of God in the Old Testament, preached a mixture of visual images, spiritual insight, and a call for divine obedience. In the time of the Babylonians' exile, Ezekiel had a grueling job of preaching to the audience, who were worn out and incarcerated. The portrayal of prophetic visions in his works, sometimes fantastical and symbolic, conveyed divine messages that surpassed the immediacy of the context. The prophetic visions of the prophets were often messages from God that went beyond that current time. Ezekiel's role was, however, not limited to warnings of future events. He served as a mentor, spurring the people to be more repentant and renew their faith in the Lord.

The Book of Ezekiel, among others, manifests in prophecies, visions, and symbolic activities. It deals with godly rerun, revitalization, and God's power in world affairs. The Prophet Ezekiel, in the passage about the valley of the dry bones, artistically points out that, even in seemingly hopeless situations, there is a possibility of spiritual renewal and resurrection. Not only does Ezekiel provide a unique and imaginative vision of the restored temple, but this vision also represents the fact that the divine presence of God is once again among the people. This vision was a light on the path ahead, manifesting a trust that God was steadfastly pursuing His covenant despite the tribulations of exile.

EZEKIEL 48:28

28 'The southern boundary of Gad will run south from Tamar to the waters of Meribah Kadesh, then along the Wadi of Egypt to the Mediterranean Sea.

29 'This is the land you are to allot as an inheritance to the tribes of Israel, and these will be their portions,' declares the Sovereign LORD.

The gates of the new city

30 'These will be the exits of the city: begin-ning on the north side, which is 4,500 cubits long, 31 the gates of the city will be named after the tribes of Israel. The three gates on the north side will be the gate of Reuben, the gate of Judah and the gate of Levi.

32 'On the east side, which is 4,500 cubits long, will be three gates: the gate of Joseph, the gate of Benjamin and the gate of Dan.

The Book of Ezekiel.[29]

Ezekiel, a watchman whose reverence for his mission is unmatched, is unshakable in his commitment. He was always determined to deliver his messages, even when confronted with opposition. Today, his messages, just like the others, continue to ring true, serving as a timeless reproach for those who have grown complacent in their spiritual lives and offering reassurance through divine reinstatement and hope. His book is a reflection of his experience, character, and guidance that is still useful in finding oneself and inner peace today.

Daniel: The Interpreter of Dreams

Daniel, a figure of distinction among the major prophets, emerged as a beacon of faith and resilience in the Old Testament. His significance goes beyond the length of his book, showing his unwavering commitment to God amid challenging circumstances. During the Babylonian exile, Daniel's life in the royal court shows him facing trials and temptations. His steadfast devotion to God and refusal to compromise his principles, as seen in the story of the lion's den, exemplifies his unwavering faith. The Book of Daniel is a mix of prophecies, dreams, and historical accounts. Daniel's interpretation of King Nebuchadnezzar's dream and the subsequent visions offers profound insights into God's divine plan. The prophetic passages, including the vision of the four beasts and the seventy weeks, glimpses into future events with remarkable precision.

The debate surrounding Daniel's classification as a major prophet adds complexity to his legacy. While in many Christian traditions, Daniel is considered a major prophet, the Hebrew Bible often places him among the writers rather than the prophets. His life exemplifies resilience in the face of adversity. From his early days in Babylon to encounters with powerful rulers, he consistently relies on God's guidance. His unwavering trust is encapsulated in the well-known story of the fiery furnace, where he and his companions emerge unscathed, which is a testament to God's divine protection.

In a contemporary context, his life encourages Christians to stand firm in their faith, even in challenging situations. His experiences remain timeless lessons on integrity, prayer, and trust in God's providence.

The Minor Prophets

The Minor Prophets, a collection of twelve concise yet powerful books in the Old Testament, constitute a diverse and often overlooked segment of biblical prophecy. Unlike the major prophets, whose extensive writings dominate the prophetic landscape, the minor prophets offer profound insights into compact narratives. These prophetic voices, Hosea, Joel, Amos, Obadiah, Jonah, Micah, Nahum, Habakkuk, Zephaniah, Haggai, Zechariah, and Malachi, collectively contribute to a rich form of messages that address diverse themes such as justice, repentance, and the coming redemption.

Spanning through different historical periods and addressing different audiences, the minor prophets convey divine messages with a concise yet impactful eloquence. Their writings delve into the intricate dynamics of God's covenant relationship with His people, revealing the consequences of disobedience and the enduring hope of restoration. Despite their brevity, the minor prophets played a significant role in the broader prophetic tradition, complementing the narratives of their major counterparts. Each prophet contributed a unique perspective, capturing the uniqueness of their respective historical contexts while conveying timeless truths that resonate with humanity's enduring struggles and aspirations.

As you explore the collective wisdom embedded in these brief yet potent books, you will get to unveil a beautiful picture of prophecies that speak to the intricate interplay between the sovereignty of God and human responsibility. These prophets, although considered minor due to the length of their books, were major contributors to the prophetic parts that echoed throughout the Old Testament and in today's world as well.

Hosea

Hosea, a minor prophet in the Old Testament, led a life that illustrated God's love and human frailty. God asked him to marry Gomer, a woman of unfaithfulness, meaning a harlot. Hosea's struggles mirrored Israel's spiritual unfaithfulness to God. Despite Gomer's infidelity, Hosea's unwavering commitment became a living metaphor for God's enduring love towards a nation known for its perpetual unfaithfulness. Hosea's prophetic ministry extended beyond his marital metaphor. His messages, often accompanied by visions, emphasized the consequences of Israel's spiritual adultery and called for repentance. The prophet's life exemplified God's redemptive yearning, culminating in the symbolic act of purchasing Gomer back after her descent into slavery.

In the face of personal heartbreak, Hosea's obedience conveyed a timeless message of God's relentless pursuit of His people. His life stands as a constant testimony to the transformative power of God's love, urging all to heed the call to repentance and embrace the enduring grace of God's faithfulness.

Joel

Joel, as a minor prophet, was a voice of significance in the Old Testament. He delivered a concise yet powerful message centered on repentance, God's judgment, and restoration. Although very little is known about his personal life, the timelessness of his message extends beyond the pages of his book. Joel's focus on the day of the Lord and future judgment was illustrated with a locust plague, and in urging repentance amidst calamity, he emphasizes the importance of turning to God. He envisioned a restoration of God's blessings upon genuine repentance, revealing God as a merciful and gracious deity. Despite the brevity of his book, Joel emerges as a significant voice, urging his audience to recognize the profound consequences of their actions and embrace the promise of divine restoration through heartfelt repentance.

Amos

Amos, a shepherd-turned-prophet, arises as a formidable voice among the minor prophets in the Old Testament. This is due to the grand content of his messages, regardless of the size of the book. His messages, delivered during a period of affluence and moral decay in Israel, condemn social injustice and religious hypocrisy. Amos boldly proclaims God's judgment against nations, including Israel, emphasizing that true worship extends beyond the rituals they practiced and has more to do with justice and righteousness. Despite his humble beginnings, Amos confronted kings and priests without fear, denouncing exploitation and calling for repentance. His visions, including the plumb line and the basket of ripe fruit, vividly illustrate impending judgment. Amos's enduring relevance lies in his uncompromising call for social equality and genuine devotion, challenging Christians to align their actions with God's standards of justice and righteousness.

Obadiah

Obadiah, although being the shortest book in the Old Testament, is loved by many Christians. Its concise nature and deep message resonate with the Christian life. Popular verses like Obadiah 1:17, "But upon mount Zion shall be deliverance, and there shall be holiness, and the house of Jacob shall possess their possessions." are often used today. This book presents a profound message through its minor prophet. In addressing the nation of Edom, Obadiah delivers a stern warning about impending judgment due to their pride, violence, and betrayal towards their brother nation, Israel. The prophet unveils a vision of Edom's downfall, emphasizing divine retribution for their arrogance and mistreatment of Israel during times of distress.

Despite Edom's lofty mountain strongholds, Obadiah prophesies their ultimate humiliation. This short yet impactful book serves as a stark reminder that pride and injustice will not go unnoticed by a just and sovereign God. Obadiah's message goes beyond the specific historical context, urging everyone to reflect on the consequences of arrogance and cruelty while highlighting God's commitment to justice and the protection of His people.

Jonah

The life of Jonah, as humorous as it is, is full of lessons. Jonah tried outsmarting God out of fear, like so many today, trying to act smart to get God to bend His will or plan for one reason or another – for Jonah, it was fear. He was instructed by God to prophesy against the city of Nineveh but attempted to escape this divine calling. In the process, God trapped him in the belly of a fish, where he repented, and when he was released, he fulfilled God's command. Jonah's story emphasizes God's compassion for repentant hearts when He forgave the people of Nineveh due to their genuinely remorseful response following Jonah's message. The prophet's initial reluctance and God's patient correction reveal a broader message about God's universal concern for everyone.

Jonah's unique narrative serves as a compelling reminder of God's grace. It challenges Christians to embrace His mercy and extend it to others beyond personal biases and prejudices.

Micah

Micah, one of the minor prophets of the Old Testament, delivers a powerful message that focuses on themes of justice, humility, and hope. He was born in a rural setting and grew up to become a strong voice against corruption and oppression in both Samaria and Jerusalem. His prophecies condemn social injustice, exposing the mistreatment of the poor and vulnerable. Micah foresees a future where God's justice prevails, and peace emanates from Zion. His famous words, "Act justly, love mercy, and walk humbly with your God," capture the essence of his prophetic message. Micah's vision extends beyond his time, urging nations to pursue righteousness and recognize the enduring hope found in God's redemptive plan, ultimately pointing toward the arrival of the Messiah in Bethlehem, as foretold by this humble shepherd-prophet.

Nahum

Nahum is regarded as a prophet of doom and deliverance. He emerged as a powerful voice among the minor prophets in the Old Testament. His focus was on the impending judgment against Nineveh, the capital of the Assyrian Empire. Nahum vividly describes the city's imminent downfall, portraying God as both a jealous avenger and a refuge for those who trust in Him. The Prophet's striking imagery includes clear depictions of nature's forces and divine retribution, emphasizing the consequences of Nineveh's oppressive reign. Nahum's message, delivered with poetic intensity, reassures the oppressed and warns the oppressors. Despite its seemingly harsh tone, Nahum's prophecy showed the balance between divine justice and compassion, revealing God's commitment to justice and the protection of His people in the face of ruthless tyranny.

Habakkuk

Habakkuk engages in a unique dialogue with God, addressing the perplexities of injustice and divine response. His story and life happened in a time of societal turmoil. Habakkuk questions God's apparent silence in the face of wickedness. In a profound exchange, God unveils His plan, assuring that justice will prevail. This shows that as a Christian, you can always talk to God and be sure that He will respond. Habakkuk's journey from doubt to trust was shown in his powerful prayer and affirmation of faith. The Prophet's name means "embrace" or "wrestle," symbolizing his intimate struggle with God. Despite the uncertainty, Habakkuk emerges with an unwavering trust in God's sovereignty, proclaiming that, even in the absence of visible prosperity, he will rejoice in the Lord. Habakkuk's dialogue exemplifies the authenticity of wrestling with faith and finding strength in surrender to God's unfathomable wisdom and providence.

Zephaniah

Zephaniah, a prophet during Josiah's reign, delivers a powerful message against Judah's corruption. Connected to Hezekiah, he rebukes societal sins, warning of God's imminent judgment. The prophet vividly describes the "Day of the Lord," urging repentance. Just like Obadiah, he condemns arrogance and pride, emphasizing humility. Amid stern warnings, he foretells a remnant finding refuge in God, which offers a glimpse of hope. His poetic expressions capture the judgment's severity and the promise of restoration. Beyond the immediate context, Zephaniah anticipates ultimate redemption through the Messiah. In a morally decayed era, Zephaniah challenges individuals to seek righteousness, humility, and a genuine relationship with God. His timeless words call for repentance and refuge in the Lord's mercy.

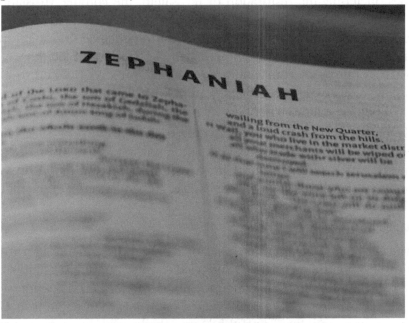

The Book of Zephaniah.[30]

Haggai

Another favorite of many is the book of Haggai. Haggai was a post-exilic prophet, but despite this, he emerged as a focused messenger with a message to rebuild the ruined temple of Jerusalem. He spoke about the people's neglect of the house of their God amid their surpluses and abundance. Haggai then called for a renewed commitment to reconstruct the temple, linking national blessings to obedience. He emphasized the importance of prioritizing God's dwelling place while promising divine favor upon their efforts. His strategic leadership plays a crucial role in motivating Zerubbabel, the governor, and Joshua, the high priest, to resume temple construction despite challenges.

Through Haggai's exhortations, the people rekindled their commitment to God's house. The completion of the second temple attests to Haggai's impact and symbolizes the restoration of worship and divine presence.

Zechariah

Zechariah, also a post-exilic prophet, collaborates with Haggai to inspire the reconstruction of the temple in Jerusalem. His prophecies, delivered in symbolic visions and clear oracles, cover a broad spectrum of themes, including the restoration of Jerusalem, the coming Messiah, and the future kingdom of God. Zechariah's visionary messages blend encouragement with stern warnings, urging repentance and a return to God's ways. The prophet's emphasis on the dual roles of the coming Messiah, a humble servant and a conquering king, contributed to a rich Messianic imagery. He envisioned a purified and reunited Jerusalem, one that symbolized a future era of divine restoration.

Zechariah's prophecies, while deeply rooted in the post-exilic period, extend beyond that time, offering a panoramic view of God's redemptive plan. His words resonate with Christians, prompting reflection on God's faithfulness, the significance of repentance, and anticipation of the ultimate fulfillment of Messianic promises.

Malachi

Malachi, the concluding prophet of the Old Testament, addressed a post-exilic community that struggled with spiritual apathy and compromised worship. His name, meaning "my messenger," underscores his role as a divine messenger. Malachi confronts the people with God's enduring love and their unfaithfulness, challenging them to return to genuine worship. Through a series of dialogues, Malachi addresses issues like priestly corruption, marital infidelity, and offerings lacking sincerity. He anticipates the coming of a messenger preparing the way for the Lord and a prophetic nod to John the Baptist preceding Jesus. Malachi's messages revealed God's desire for heartfelt devotion and faithfulness. His prophecies echo themes of repentance, restoration, and divine intervention. His conclusion solidifies the Old Testament, emphasizing the importance of obedience and a faithful remnant. His words today urge Christians to examine their devotion and embrace the transformative power of God's enduring love.

Moment of Reflection

1. Consider the historical context of the prophetic books. In which ways do the societal challenges faced by the prophets mirror or differ from challenges in today's world?

2. Reflect on the role of repentance in the prophetic messages. How does the concept of turning back to God apply to your own life?

3. Explore the recurring themes of judgment and restoration in the prophetic books. How do these themes provide a framework for understanding God's interaction with His people?

4. Consider the Messianic prophecies found in the prophets. How do these prophecies shape your understanding of Jesus Christ and His significance?

5. Reflect on the messages of hope and redemption in the prophetic books. How can these messages inspire resilience and faith in the face of adversity?

6. Consider the relevance of the prophets' calls for social justice and care for the marginalized in today's society. How do these teachings affect your actions and attitudes?

7. Reflect on the personal journeys and struggles of the prophets. How do their experiences with God's call and correction relate to your spiritual journey?

8. Consider the overarching theme of God's faithfulness throughout the prophetic books. How does this theme impact your understanding of God's character and your relationship with Him?

It has been hundreds of years since these prophets lived and their books were written, but their words still hold deep truth today. That's the amazing thing about the Bible; it's a living, breathing book that continues to speak into the lives of those who would have it. As you read further into the books of the prophets, keep an open heart and mind, and ask God to reveal any area of your life that needs adjustment and transformation.

Chapter 9: The Historical Books: From Joshua to Esther

Other books of the Bible also address events that happened in the past, but these books you are about to read contain some of the most fascinating stories that shape a Christian's early life. They contain an array of events, ranging from shifts in leadership, kingdom divisions, royal reigns, exiles, triumphant returns, love stories, etc. This chapter will guide you through all these events by simplifying the tales and bringing life into the characters and their impact on a Christian's faith. You mustn't approach these books as another history text or an enjoyable fictional novel, but rather as a detailed account of the lives of people who once walked on this earth, having real feelings and emotions and their crosses and burdens to bear. They were regular

They were regular men and women just like you, with real-life challenges and temptations, flaws, and weaknesses.[31]

men and women just like you, with real-life challenges and temptations, flaws, and weaknesses. Still, they chose to yield and surrender their wills to God, even in seasons when it seemed impossible. They are reflections of human courage, faith, and divine intervention. As you move through these pages, open your heart to receive wisdom and inspiration for your life.

What Are These Books About?

These historical books are more than just people, places, and events; they embody broader themes that resonate with other parts of the Bible. Five major themes can be drawn from them: God's sovereignty, presence, promises, kingdom, and covenant. Here is a more detailed look into each theme:

1. **God's Sovereignty:** The historical books consistently portray God as sovereign over all, from nature to the affairs of nations. His authority is demonstrated through miracles and requires Israel's submission.

2. **God's Presence:** Throughout these books, God was intimately involved in the affairs of men. He appointed leaders like Joshua, judges in times of distress, and chose kings. His closeness is evident in the assistance provided to godly kings and prophets. Yet, at times, his presence seems obscured, often linked to Israel's sin or, in some cases, a deliberate act.

3. **God's Promises:** The historical books, especially those echoing the themes of the Pentateuch (Five Books), leave no doubt that Abraham carried the promise and that the promise outlived him. This promise - called the "Abrahamic Covenant" - constituted of land possession, children proliferation, and blessing, was primarily fulfilled in Joshua's time.

4. **God's Covenant:** The Abrahamic Covenant implied that conformity to the Lord's commandments was a very serious human duty, demonstrated by the faithfulness of Abraham. Another covenant called the Mosaic Covenant will then arise to govern life per the past covenant that promised rewards for righteousness and punishment for unrighteousness, which is frequently depicted in historical books.

5. **God's Kingdom:** The sovereign power of God is reflected explicitly in His rule over the world but also implicitly through earthly kings. They served as God's representatives on earth,

entrusted with His kingdom, as depicted in texts like 2 Chronicles 13, Zech. 7:9 and 1 Chron. 29:5.

The Historical Books

Below are the books from Joshua to Esther:

Joshua

In the Book of Joshua, the seasoned leadership of Moses was replaced by the courageous leadership of Joshua. This section symbolizes a decisive point in human history, which was just before the Israelites entered the promised land to fight and claim their inheritance. The story opens with the death of Moses, the celebrated guide who led the Israelites through the desert. Now, the leadership role was given to Joshua, a consecrated follower of Moses. The book of Joshua records the whole journey of the Israelites to Canaan, a land dedicated to them by God. The whole story is centered on the crossing of the Jordan River, a miraculous event depicting the parting of the Red Sea in the time of Moses, the fall of Jericho walls, and the sun remaining motionless at Joshua's command during a difficult battle. These deeds were the results of obedience and divine intervention in the wake of the Israelites, and they also signify God's presence with them. The book also describes some territories that were allotted to the twelve tribes in the process of settling in Canaan, which served as a blueprint for the Israelites. The address comes to a close with a solemn covenant established between the people and a faithful God.

The Book of Joshua depicts the importance of having unswerving faith and remaining faithful when dealing with God. The life of Joshua lays out the foundation for the other biblical accounts, reminding us of how legacy is built on trust in God and staying true to one's principles.

Judges

The Book of Judges comes up as a thrilling sequel to Joshua, detailing the turbulent times of the past in Israel. While employing the Promised Land as a narrative background, the book follows a sequence of chronicles from the moment of capture to the time of oppression and the cycle of actions and reactions, the time of the judges. While the Israelites settled into their designated areas, God appointed different judges, charismatic and dedicated people, to guide and lead them to freedom from oppression. These judges, such as Gideon, Samson, and Deborah, played a key role in the lives of the Israelites. The Book of Judges highlights the culture and politics of that time. It portrays a society dealing with the human complexities of being faithful. In their constant struggle for power amidst the ups and downs of their victories and defeats, the Israelites also deal with the problem of coexistence with neighboring people and the attraction of gods of other tribes. The entry of each judge is the resounding echo of the nation's call for liberation, portraying a manifestation of divine acts amid human imperfection.

The Book of Judges.[32]

The cycle of rebellion, oppression, repentance, and miraculous intervention of God reveals the spiritual and moral tests suffered by the Israelites. The Book of Judges, beyond the historical collection, is a grand examination of human nature. It reveals the issues around the aspirations of a people endeavoring to stick to their covenant with God. It is a colorful picture of the typical human experience: flawed leadership, social turmoil, and the everlasting faithfulness of a forgiving God. This era of the judges paved the way for more profound discourses on the maze of divine-human relations and the endless quest for justice and righteousness. Some of these judges were:

- **Deborah:** Deborah, a prophetess and judge, defied societal norms with unwavering faith. Her wise counsel and leadership guided Israel to victory against the Canaanites. She is known for the pivotal role she played in securing Israel's freedom.

- **Samson:** Samson, marked by incredible strength and Nazirite vows, grappled with personal weaknesses. Despite his flaws, his exploits against the Philistines showcased God's power working through human frailty. His life revealed the consequences of succumbing to temptation.

- **Jephthah:** Jephthah rose from an outcast to a judge. His vow, resulting in his daughter's sacrifice, epitomized the complexities of devotion and the human cost of rash promises. His leadership secured a brief rest for Israel.

- **Gideon:** Gideon, initially doubtful, became a courageous leader. He led a small army to defeat the large Midianites army. His story highlights the transformative power of faith and God's ability to use unlikely individuals.

- **Ehud:** Ehud, a left-handed judge, orchestrated a daring assassination of Moab's oppressive King, Eglon. His strategic and decisive action liberated Israel from Moabite oppression, exemplifying God's unexpected deliverance.

- **Othniel:** Being Israel's first judge, he rose to prominence by defeating the Mesopotamians. His leadership set a precedent for the judges who followed because of his faithfulness to God. Othniel exemplified the importance of obedience in securing God's deliverance.

Ruth

The Book of Ruth shows God's faithfulness, salvation, and favor through the eyes of the main character, Ruth, after whom the book is named. The events in this book took place at a time when judges still governed God's people. That aside, it was also a troubling time for the Israelites as they faced intense agricultural problems. The story starts with Naomi's family leaving for the Moab lands because of a great famine that has already affected the lands of Israel. Tragedy strips Naomi of her spouse and sons, rendering her childless. Ruth, Naomi's daughter-in-law, decides to cling to her in her trying times when she declares, "The people you like should be my people, and the God you worship should be my God also." Ruth 1:16-17. Ruth and Naomi moved back to Bethlehem, struggling financially as widows and working on the gleaners' rows to survive. Ruth earns the admiration of Boaz, who later marries her and brings redemption to her mother-in-law.

Culturally, Ruth provides a glimpse into Israelite customs, kinship ties, and the practice of kinsman-redeemer responsibilities. The story reflects societal expectations, economic challenges, and the resilience of individuals navigating uncertain times. Also, Ruth's action suggests how a person's choice matters in the larger story of life, as well as destiny. The story is one of hope in God to make restitutions. The main theme is the combination of individual strife, societal actions, and the ever-present guidance of God.

1st and 2nd Samuel

The books of 1st and 2nd Samuel, which embody the historical narrative of ancient Israel time, document a complicated phase of evolution from the season of God being their only king to the establishment of earthly kingship. The main characters are Samuel, the last judge; Saul, a central prophet and Israel's first king; and David, the most important figure. David started as a shepherd boy and ended up as a king and an iconic person in Israel's history. The story began with the account of Samuel's birth and his subsequent selection as a messenger of God. However, amidst the people's request for the appointment of an earthly ruler, God instructs Samuel to anoint Saul as the first king of Israel.

Culturally, these books reveal Israelite religious practices, the society around them, and the family (clan) as the base of their life. It reveals the Jewish people's attempts to form a centralized governing structure while simultaneously confronting external threats and domestic fragmentation. The story depicts the disagreement between the tribal way of life and the rise of a new monarchy. It shows how the tribal culture was strengthened against any changes, especially those related to the governmental system. In the book, you will be shown the challenges that come with leadership and the outcomes of not obeying God's orders. Saul's reign is noted for its achievements and defeats, leading to a protracted process for him to secure his power and preserve the Israelite covenant. The ascent of David marks a new epoch in the history of Israel through bravery, craftiness, and favor of God.

Both books are highly linked to the Israelite's resilience toward political intrigues and spiritual rebirth. The tales of Samuel, Saul, and David are timeless stories that teach us about leadership, faithfulness, and God's power in a nation's affairs.

1st and 2nd Kings

The books of 1st and 2nd Kings are the history books that continued where the books of 1st and 2nd Samuel left off. These books handed out a detailed account of the monarchy period by presenting the kings' reigns and Elijah's and Elisha's prophetic ministries. This book gives its readers an overview of the political, cultural, and religious situations of ancient Israel. You will come across different kings of the kingdom of Israel and Judah whose performance is benchmarked by their obedience to the Lord's statutes.

Concerning culture, these books talk about Jewish religious practices, social codes, and their belief in one true God, which was often corrupted with idolatry. The general theme of these books was the continuous conflict the Kings of Israel had within themselves on total loyalty to God and their attraction to the foreign gods. One after the other, they faced the same struggles as they aimed to establish a covenant with God.

Both books provide a stark view of what happens if leaders happen to engage in wrongdoing. The storyline reflects the cycle of apostasy, God's wrath, and God's restoration of Israel. With a focus on royal succession and court politics, the books tackle the ideas of power, loyalty, and the lasting repercussions of men's actions. In the end, the books of the 1st and 2nd Kings deliver a cautionary teaching but at the same time testify to the sincerity of God, who remains faithful despite human imperfections.

1st and 2nd Chronicles

The first and second books of Chronicles provide a different story of the history of Israel from the Bible. These books deal with genealogies, culture, and the reigns of different kings, giving a detailed insight into the country. The 1st Chronicles is opened by genealogies covering the descendants from Adam to the Davidic line, and the promise of God is seen in the continuity of the chain. This is followed by a section devoted to the Davidic reign, where his pattern of kingship was described as one based on worship. Solomon's auspicious reign, which fulfilled the construction of the Temple, was the most prominent event, and it was elaborated extensively with a focus on all the religious rituals.

The Book of Chronicles 1.[83]

Ceremonially, these books are focused on the importance of worship, the role of the priesthood, and the significance of God's law within the culture of faith. The First Book of Chronicles presents an idealized view of Israel's history, in which most of it emphasizes the spiritual aspects and the persistence of the covenant cords. The theological agenda of the chronicler (referring to the writer of the book) aspires to worship God wisely and stay loyal to the right person. In political terms, 1st and 2nd

Chronicles replay the monarchy period, stressing the kingships of David and Solomon and continuing to trace the rulers of Judah. The chronicler passes his judgment on every monarch according to their devotion to the Lord and compliance with the covenant. The explanation reveals the theological interpretation of historical reality, emphasizing the political consequences of obedience and disobedience.

In summary, 1st and 2nd Chronicles are meant to be a theological reflection of Israel's history as they are focused on faithfulness to God and righteous leadership. The Bible keeps on calling on people to renew their relationship with God by reminding them that God's commitments are everlasting. Chronicles provides a novel perspective on the Israelites' battling experiences and their hopes, setting them up for spiritual contemplation and strengthening their faith in God.

Ezra

The book of Ezra, a sequel to the historical accounts from the 2nd Chronicles, focuses on the events surrounding the re-emergence of Jewish exiles from Babylon and back to Jerusalem. The priest, Ezra, becomes the leading character in the restoration plans with a primary focus on the revival of their spiritual life. The scenario is set in the time of the Persian Empire and the royal decree of King Cyrus to Jews in Babylon, which allowed them to return to their homeland. Culture-wise, Ezra emphasizes maintaining their religious identity and keeping the law of God. The rebuilding of the Temple comes to represent God's restoration of the relationship between the Children of Israel and Himself and the return to the way of worship. The book underlines the issues faced by the repatriates, such as the opposition of neighboring communities and internal conflicts.

Politically, Ezra faced complications working under the Persians. It shows the conflict between the demands of Jewish liberty and compliance with the Greek rulers, as Ezra aimed at fostering a community based on a commitment to the laws of God. The book of Ezra stands as a witness to God's faithfulness in answering prayers of restoration and redemption. The exiles' comeback is a turning point in Israel's history, ushering in the earliest phase of a fresh cycle in the nation's connection with God. Through the actions of Ezra and the other leaders, the Jewish people underwent a spiritual revival. They rekindled their faithfulness to the Covenant of God.

In summary, Ezra conveys a strong message about the hardships and dreams of the Israelites as they struggle to restore their country and strive for a better life. The story is a testament to the significance of faithfulness, perseverance, and reliance on God's mercy in hard times.

Nehemiah

The book of Nehemiah is the closure of the narrative of the restoration of the Jews after their exile to Babylon and the structure of the construction of the walls of Jerusalem, which happened under the supervision of Nehemiah. Nehemiah, the King's cupbearer in Persia, was permitted to return to Jerusalem to oversee the rebuilding project. Nehemiah indicates the importance of loyalty and faith in God during a difficult period. The reconstruction of the walls, on the other hand, symbolizes the city of Jerusalem's security and the safety of its people. Nehemiah's leadership should be highlighted as a fundamental component of successful governance and the enhancement of local leaders in the process of reducing social and economic challenges.

Politically, Nehemiah goes through the difficulties of governing under Persian dominion by making sure the expectations of the imperial government are correlated with those of the Jewish community. The biblical account portrays Nehemiah as a skilled administrator and diplomat who actively sought peace with surrounding enemies and executed reforms that focused on ending injustice and inequality. The book of Nehemiah is a chronicle of the Jewish people's steadfastness and obduracy in remaking their land and restoring their religions. The storyline is a display of the hardships and hopes of the Israelites as they strive to return Jerusalem to its former grandeur and revive their relationships with God.

In light of all these, Nehemiah reveals lessons about the problems of building a state and the significance of a visionary leader during critical times. A story like this will encourage you to keep pushing, even through the darkness, and to continue the fight for restoration that involves justice, security, and spiritual renewal. With Nehemiah's example, the book thus reveals the vital role of faith, endurance, and divine grace in bringing in lasting reforms.

Esther

The Book of Esther is set in the 5th-century Persian Empire when the Jews were scattered all over the world. It follows a brilliant story of Jews in the era. The story takes place in the capital city of Susa, where King

Xerxes rules a highly resourceful empire that extends from India to Cush. The central figures of the story are Esther, a Jewish orphan who became queen, her cousin and guardian Mordecai, and a Jewish slayer, Haman.

In the cultural aspect, Esther reveals the struggles of keeping the Judaism identity and commitment in a foreign environment. The story delves into issues of assimilation and resistance when Esther has to hide her true identity despite her participation in the court functions. Mordecai's refusal to show respect to the King's right-hand man, Haman, propels a series of events that culminate in the plot to eradicate all the Jews.

The Book of Esther revealed the processes of power and maneuvering that occurred within the Persian court. As Xerxes, the King, becomes impressed with Haman, a prominent official carrying the torch of his hatred against Mordecai and the Jews, the dangers of minority communities before the political schemes are highlighted. Esther's courage in preventing the planned massacre by Haman showed that there could be a turning point in the path of a nation's history through the daring act of one single person. Esther's book, in a way, sets the stage for the subsequent questions about what it means to be Jewish in exile, what is required for the survival of the Jewish people in the hostile environment, and how God cares about His people in troubled waters. Purim, the festival that celebrates the very same deliverance of the Jewish people and their enduring importance to the Jews, is celebrated on the 14th and 15th days of February.

In general, the Book of Esther describes a striking story of defiance, resistance, and divine presence amid challenging circumstances. This story is a universal lesson about faithfulness, strong bonds, and eliminating injustice, which are the values that the readers have always appreciated. Through the eyes of Esther and Mordecai's situation, the story encourages hope and perseverance during the period of uncertainty and oppression.

Moment Of Reflection

1. When you think about the significance of covenants, how can understanding these agreements influence your commitment to God?

2. Considering leadership roles, how might you apply or avoid aspects of the leadership styles seen in the historical kings in your areas of influence?

3. Reflecting on God's promises, how can the assurance of His commitments influence your outlook and decisions, especially during times of uncertainty?

4. Reflect on instances in your life when you felt God's presence. How can you nurture a more conscious awareness of His closeness in your daily experiences?

5. When you consider themes of obedience and disobedience, how do the characters' choices prompt self-reflection on your responses to God's guidance in various situations?

The historical books, however, identified several themes and consistently maintained a general theme that reveals God's continuous fulfillment of His promise to be with His children. The stories captured in these books were not just for historical or theological knowledge but to open the heart of every reader to God and His intentions. The Bible remains the best place to go to get the most from these stories.

Chapter 10: How the Old and New Testament Link

At this point, you already know that the Bible is one big, unified piece from the very start of Genesis until the end of Malachi. The Old Testament prepared the stage and laid the foundation for the good news that the New Testament brings. The New Testament is more figurative; it puts together everything the Old Testament has been trying to tell you. It is impossible not to see how the Holy Spirit divinely inspired the Bible, as it contains everything you need for your life. Every book from the Old to the New Testament is so beautifully interwoven. They complement each other, from the creation of Adam to the coming of Jesus, the Prophets of old to the Apostles of the early Church, etc. It is one grand tale of different

The Bible will only make sense by merging the Old Testament with the New Testament.[34]

dispensations whose relevance and significance transcends time, and its lessons are still very much applicable in today's world.

One section would be incomplete without the other: having the New without the Old just wouldn't be right, and vice versa; there would be too many unfilled gaps and missing pieces. The Bible will only make sense by merging both parts; you cannot rule out one from the other. As a matter of fact, most of Jesus's teaching and that of his apostles always consisted of references from the Old Testament, and this isn't hard to figure out as modern-day Bibles come with cross-references that point from the Old Testament to the New and the other way around. Nevertheless, the unison between these two sections is bigger than this; the Bible is not just about the story told by the Old Testament, which was later brought to life by Christ in the New Testament. It tells of God's unending love, seen in His unrelenting pursuit of humanity, a pursuit of love that brought about the fulfillment of the promise of Jesus Christ as the savior of the world.

This chapter is here to help you simplify the link between the two sections of the Bible, identify similar themes, compare and contrast both themes based on their usage in the different sections, and have a better and more grounded understanding of the Bible in general.

The Link

It is necessary to understand the link between the Old Testament and the New Testament to help you lay a perspective in your Christian walk and know your place and role in the body of Christ. All through the Old Testament, only the people of Israel were regarded as God's chosen people. However, that changed with the coming of Jesus Christ in the New Testament, which brought about a reconciliation between you and God. However, walking under the New Covenant does not diminish the importance of the Old Testament, but rather, a focused look at both sections, side by side, will bring you a better understanding of your place and inheritance as a believer and a child of God. The New Testament is the fulfillment of the promise made in the Old Testament, and you can't do one without the other.

The Bible is a single story with two parts, the Old and New Testaments, both working together. They validate each other because they share a common author—God. Although different people physically wrote the Bible, they did so under the inspiration of the Holy Spirit. In 2 Peter 1:21, it's stated that holy men spoke as the Holy Spirit moved them. This emphasizes that every word in the Bible comes from divine inspiration.

Further confirming this, 2 Timothy 3:16 declares that all Scripture is given by the inspiration of God, serving various purposes. When you understand this, you will realize that God, as the divine author, had a central goal; the revelation of Christ to every Christian. Jesus Himself pointed this out in John 5:39, stating that the Scriptures testify about Him. So, even though you encounter Jesus directly in the New Testament, His presence has been there from the very beginning of the Bible. The central message all through the books has been Christ, making the Bible a cohesive revelation of God's plan for His people. Without the knowledge of the fall of man, their feeble attempts to reconcile back to God, the generation's worth of efforts made, the promise of a better way, and the anticipation of the fulfillment of that promise, the New Testament would not have as much significance as it does today. A new Christian must get to see where it all began, how one event led to another, and how it relates to them.

So, here are some core themes, events, people, and things that took place in the Old Testament that find more emphasis in the New Testament:

Exploring the Connection Between Old and New Testaments

The Old Testament and the New Testament may seem like separate books, but they are deeply connected. This section will take you through how the practices, laws, and ceremonies from the old days will help you understand the big picture of God's plan.

Old Testament Practices Fulfilled in the New Testament

Back in the time of the Old Testament, the children of Israel followed a system of offering animal sacrifices to make up for their sins and obtain a right standing with God. These sacrifices were tedious, as they required specific rules and rituals in Mosaic Law for each of them. Besides that, they still couldn't achieve a perfect goal of total cleanliness, as these sacrifices had to be made over and over again. Due to this, the New Testament was made to usher in a one-time change in the ways of achieving cleanliness and righteousness in the Old Testament. The old way of sacrificing animals finds its ultimate meaning and completion in the work of Jesus Christ. He is often called the "Lamb of God" because His sacrifice on the cross became the perfect offering that fulfills the purpose of animal sacrifices once and for all. The Bible says in Hebrews 9:11-12 that "Jesus, by his blood, secured eternal redemption" – this means forgiveness and a restored relationship with God. The very thing they tried so hard to establish and keep in the Old Testament was finally made available. For clarity, Jesus didn't come to get rid of the Old Testament rules but to fulfill them; this He explained in Matthew 5:17. His sacrifice on the cross totally replaces the need for animal sacrifices, and this is a big deal because it's a one-time sacrifice for all.

His sacrifice on the cross totally replaces the need for animal sacrifices, and this is a big deal because it's a one-time sacrifice for all.[33]

The New Testament makes it clear that the sacrifice of Jesus is different from the old animal sacrifices, which only had a temporary impact and a symbol of something better to come. The sacrifice on the cross was a complete and final solution to the problem of sin. In Hebrews 10:19-20. The

The Bible, in Hebrews 10:19-20, encourages Christians to confidently approach God because of the sacrifice of Jesus. His sacrifice opens up a new way for everyone to connect with God. In summary, the Old Testament practice of sacrificing animals finds fulfillment in the person and work of Jesus. His sacrifice on the cross brings a whole new approach for people to relate to God.

Old Testament Laws Fulfilled in the New Testament

One very common thing about the Jewish customs was the many laws they had in place: morals, ceremonial, and civil. These laws were not just for show; they were the guiding force for the children of Israel back then. It was a core part of their lives. Now, when you look at the New Testament, especially through the teachings of Jesus, you find that these laws remain, but this time, they are fulfilled in a new way. Jesus didn't come to get rid of the Old Testament laws but to show their true meaning. Somehow, the people had lost their ways and misunderstood everything He had been trying to teach them all through several generations. Because of His love, He wanted people to understand the heart and spirit behind the rules, not just to follow them externally. In Matthew 5:17, Jesus says, "I have not come to abolish the Law but to fulfill it," meaning he wanted to complete the purpose of these laws. He had to show them and everyone after them the true meaning of the law.

One core example is the command to "love your neighbor" from the Old Testament. In the New Testament, Jesus takes it a step further, teaching everyone not only to love those close to them but even their enemies (Matthew 5:43-44). This shows a shift from just following rules to letting love transform your heart – a key aspect of the fulfillment of the law in the New Testament. This means rather than carrying it out robotically, you should obey these laws out of love for God and His people. God has always been about the heart rather than the deed. The state of the heart is what matters. When your heart is compelled by love, you will gladly obey every instruction, but if not, it will only seem rigid and forced.

In the Old Testament, the laws given to the Israelites were written on stone, external, and visible. However, with the coming of the New Covenant, there is the fulfillment of the promise in a different and better way: God Himself writes His laws on your heart, emphasizing a personal relationship over external regulations. This promise was mentioned in the Old Testament book of Jeremiah 31:33. The Old Testament laws find a new and clearer understanding in the New Testament. Jesus shows you the heart behind the rules, and the New Covenant brings a personal connection with God. It's not just about following external laws; it's about letting love transform you and embracing a deeper relationship with God through the teachings of Jesus, and in doing this, you will effortlessly fulfill every law.

Old Testament Ceremonies Fulfilled in the New Testament

In the Old Testament, certain practices such as circumcision, Passover, and the Sabbath held significant roles in the religious observance of the Israelites; just like their laws, this was also a core part of the Israelites.

However, like their laws, it was done without the right understanding. As you transition into the New Testament, these practices take on a renewed and deeper meaning through the lens of Christ and the Christian faith. The Old Testament showed how they were done, but the New Testament revealed why they are done: not the reason it was done in the Old Testament, but the reason why God established it in the first place.

Circumcision, once a physical covenant marking in the Old Testament, undergoes a profound spiritual transformation in the New Testament. It was well explained in Romans 2:29 when Apostle Paul emphasized that true circumcision is a matter of the heart, achieved through faith in Christ. It shifted from being just an external ritual to a Christian's spiritual reality, which symbolizes a profound internal connection with God.

Moving to the Passover, a pivotal event commemorating the Israelites' liberation from slavery in Egypt, the New Testament reveals Jesus as the ultimate fulfillment of this Old Testament ritual. Just like circumcision, its purpose was also reinvented. In 1 Corinthians 5:7, Apostle Paul, speaking again, describes Christ as the true Passover Lamb, sacrificed for the freedom of believers from spiritual bondage. This verse helps the Christian faith to find its foundation in the deliverance brought about by Jesus' sacrificial death and His resurrection. Also, the Sabbath, a day of rest and reflection in the Old Testament, experiences a transformative fulfillment in the teachings of Jesus. In Matthew 11:28-30, Jesus invites believers to find rest not just on a specific day but continuously through a relationship with Him. He emphasizes that the Sabbath is made for man and not man for the Sabbath, as stated in Mark 2:27.

This new understanding emphasizes the Sabbath's purpose, meaning that its observation extends beyond rigid observance to a relational aspect, where Christians discover peace and renewal for their souls. The teaching reveals that the Sabbath is a gift from God intended to bring restoration and spiritual rejuvenation to humanity. Therefore, in the New Testament context, the Sabbath finds its fulfillment in Jesus, who offers a perpetual and meaningful rest that goes beyond mere adherence to a specific day.

In essence, these Old Testament practices find a richer and more profound meaning in the New Testament. Circumcision becomes a spiritual transformation of the heart through faith, Passover finds fulfillment in Jesus as the liberating Lamb, and the Sabbath evolves into a continuous spiritual rest in a relationship with Christ. These transformations show the spiritual depth that Christ brings to these ancient practices, going beyond mere rituals to a meaningful and ongoing connection with God in the Christian faith. Christ is the heart and life force of the Christian walk; everything else would be mere practices without Him.

Old Testament Feast and Festivals Fulfilled in the New Testament

Another Old Testament practice that finds fulfillment and expression in the New Testament is the feasts, like the Feast of Tabernacles and the Feast of Pentecost. These practices held special meaning as celebrations of God's faithfulness and provision; nevertheless, in the New Testament, these feasts find their fulfillment in Jesus and the events surrounding His life, death, and resurrection, and also in the outpouring of the Holy Spirit. The Feast of Tabernacles, which is a remembrance of the Israelites' journey and God's presence with them in the wilderness, finds fulfillment in the New Testament through Jesus. When it says in John 1:14 that 'the Word became flesh and dwelt among us," the term "dwelt" used in that verse can be translated as "tabernacled" or "Inhabited" from the original Greek word. This means Jesus, in His life here and after, embodies God's presence among us, providing guidance, protection, and sustenance.

The Feast of Pentecost, initially a harvest celebration, gains new meaning in the New Testament with the arrival of the Holy Spirit. In Acts 2, you see the disciples experience the Holy Spirit coming upon them, which is symbolized by tongues of fire. This event, described in Acts 2:2-4, marked the beginning of the Church and empowered Christians like yourself to share the message of Christ globally.

So, these Old Testament feasts, although a reminder of God's faithfulness, are now more than that; they point to the fulfillment of His promises in Christ. Jesus is the living embodiment of the Feast of Tabernacles, providing spiritual guidance and protection. At the same time, the Feast of Pentecost, with the Holy Spirit's arrival, signifies the birth of the Church and the ongoing presence of God with His people. In essence, these feasts are not just historical rituals. They are living symbols of God's redemptive plan. In Jesus, the promises of provision, guidance, and the Holy Spirit find their complete fulfillment. As a Christian today, you are invited to celebrate not only the past events but also the present reality of God's faithfulness in your life. These feasts were just a glimpse of what was to come; now, they brightly reflect the transformative work of Jesus and the continuous presence of the Holy Spirit in establishing and growing the Church.

The Holy Spirit's arrival signifies the birth of the Church and the ongoing presence of God with His people.[86]

Adam: The First and Second

When you look at how Old Testament practices connect with the New Testament, it's important to see how Adam and Jesus fit into the picture. The Old Testament sacrifices and rules were like a setup for Jesus to come and fix things. Jesus Christ, often called the second Adam, was not just the second; He was the last, the perfect Adam. He sorted out the mess caused by *the first Adam's* mistakes, which He did by sacrificing himself to make things right with God. A look at yourself, through the lens of Adam and Jesus, is a clear depiction of the former man, which was the old you who died to give way for the new man. Jesus didn't just talk about following the rules; He actually lived them out perfectly. This made a big difference and shows you what it means to live a good life under God's new plan. So, seeing how Jesus handled things compared to Adam is like seeing the old problems get fixed by Jesus. This whole correlation between Adam and Jesus shows you God's plan for making things right.

Moments of Reflection

1. How does the idea of Jesus as the fulfillment of Old Testament practices impact your understanding of God's plan?

2. In what ways can you relate the shift from external compliance to internal transformation, as discussed in the context of Old and New Testament laws, to your own life?

3. How might the changes to rituals in the New Testament, like circumcision, Passover, and the Sabbath, impact the way you view daily practices in your faith life?

4. Think about the similarities between Adam and Jesus regarding redemption. How does this idea connect with your personal experiences of grace and forgiveness?

5. How do you see the concept of God's promises finding fulfillment in the events of the New Testament shaping your hope and trust in God's faithfulness?

6. How does seeing Jesus as the "Lamb of God," the ultimate sacrifice, shape your ideas about forgiveness and redemption?

7. How do God's grace, love, and restoration relate to your own experiences of spiritual growth and renewal?

The connection between the Old and New Testament is that of one entity with two parts working side by side to achieve a single goal by turning promises into fulfillment, turning shadows into reality, revealing the broken and flawed areas in humanity, and fixing what is broken through Jesus Christ. The Old Testament sets things up, and the New Testament makes everything happen. It is a beautiful song of God's grace, love, and making things right again. The Old and New Testaments reflect an image of the old you and the new you.

Conclusion

As you come to the end of this book, you must reflect on the journey so far. Whether you started with burning questions, a thirst for knowledge, or just stumbled upon this book, its aim was to make your exploration of the Bible straightforward and enjoyable. In these pages, you've encountered timeless wisdom, practical lessons, and insightful stories. It revealed to you the many treasures that could easily be lost in all those words. Now, you carry with you not just information but a newfound connection with the Bible.

Now that you've scanned through the books of the Bible from Genesis to Revelation, it's not about where to begin anymore; it's about cherishing your discoveries and building on them. There is still so much to uncover, but now more than ever, you are ready to take them all on. This book doesn't just end in a one-time read; you can refer to it whenever you need a refresher or a new perspective on certain things in the Bible. This is not the conclusion of your journey but a stepping stone to a deeper understanding of the Word of God. The adventure continues with every reflection, discussion, and personal encounter with the scriptures. May the insights gained be a source of ongoing joy and inspiration in your exploration of the profound teachings found within the Bible's sacred verses, with this book always by your side whenever you seek guidance.

Part 2: Bible Study Workbook

A Beginner-Friendly Guide to Unlocking the Essentials of All 66 Books

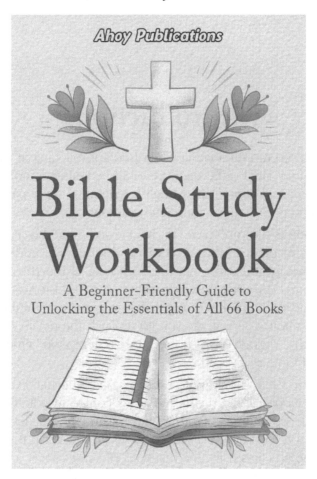

Introduction

The Bible can seem intimidating when first approaching it; staring at that thick book on the shelf gathering dust could be a little demotivating. Then you open it and find complicated English written in dense paragraphs, and after a few sentences, you get completely discouraged.

The scriptures do not have to be viewed like this complex work reserved only for the world's top scholars. With keys to understanding the text and themes running through the 66 books of the Bible, you will be seamlessly guided through the study process. As a historical and spiritual text, navigating each book's multiple layers can be a fulfilling task that reveals much about yourself. As you go through the details of each book, an overarching narrative of hope and redemption emerges as the sovereignty of God is unveiled.

Studying the Bible should not purely be an intellectual exercise. As you dive through its pages, the divine messages come alive, and your heart is realigned with worshipping God. Believers and non-believers alike can benefit from this workbook as it encourages you to grasp the Biblical text through a scholarly lens using the many lessons in its pages as a pathway to connect with the Most High. This way, a transformation into a better version of yourself is facilitated.

The workbook's theoretical aspects uncover theological, political, linguistic, and ethical meanings. The practical exercise helps you apply the text to your life in a meaningful way. Some Bible workbooks are too focused on education, while others do not provide the context to make spiritual wisdom come alive. This workbook perfectly balances the scholarly and spiritual to create a comprehensive guide that dissects every corner of the scriptures.

From the Mosaic Law and the wisdom teachings of Psalms and Proverbs to the prophetic writings and the saving grace of the Gospels, you walk along the path of a living ancient tradition. By exploring this timeless wisdom, you are reintroduced to the spiritual side of your being, awakening the reality of the God of Israel as described in the Bible.

Trace the steps of the prophets to the apostles as the covenantal system climaxes in the coming of Jesus, who died for the sins of the world. Discover the details and context of the Gospels and learn why they are still relevant in the modern world. Furthermore, unpack the intricacies of prophecy so that you can grasp the mysteries of symbolic writing and fully embrace the messages applicable today. By working diligently through the theories and activities on these pages, you will gain knowledge or a foundation to understand and embody the scripture's teachings.

Section 1: Understanding the Bible's Historical Context

The Bible is not a historical book; it is more of a *spiritual text*. However, there are historical aspects of the scriptures you must grasp to understand the book fully. Studying history can get complicated because it is not a hard science, like engineering or physics, where proof and evidence are more solid and practical.

Most history is based on archeological evidence and testimonies interpreted through various lenses. Moreover, those who wrote the texts using historical evidence also had their own views and biases. Therefore, the study in this field is robust, but many scholars disagree. This book provides the historical context of the Bible from different viewpoints to give you a complete and unbiased picture of the text. In this way, you can put the puzzle together and critically draw your own conclusions based on the available data.

The Bible is not a historical book because it is more of a spiritual text.[87]

Exploring the Bible starts by understanding that it is not only one holy book but a compilation of 66 books, depending on the canon you are looking into. For example, the Ethiopian Orthodox canon contains 81 books, significantly more than the widely accepted King James Version. Through various historical concepts and geopolitical occurrences, understanding of the Bible has shifted so it gets read differently, depending on theological schools or scholarly interpretations. Therefore, the text is living and evolving according to time and region. Sifting through these complex dynamics requires a lifetime of study. However, a snapshot can point you in the right direction to facilitate more informed opinions.

The History of the Bible

The history of the Old Testament is the establishment of an Israelite identity. The Bible will, of course, be understood differently by different readers based on the preexisting beliefs and opinions of the reader. The more literalist strain of Biblical interpretation accepts that the Exodus account of Israel becoming a nation in Egypt and the lineage of Israelites coming from Abraham is true. However, when the archeological evidence is weighed up, this narrative has problems.

The Israelite nation and its beliefs were likely an amalgamation of people who emerged from the ancient Near East. They were put in a position politically and culturally to separate themselves to establish a new nation. Clues to this view are hidden in the text, namely through the formation of the law. In Deuteronomy, there are laws like not planting different seeds on one section of land, prohibiting wearing mixed fabrics, and forbidding intermarriage with foreigners. These laws were intended to emphasize separation and solidify the establishment of a new nation from the plurality of the Western Semites.

Essentially, the Israelites are the Canaanites, although the Bible sets it up as a narrative of conquer. The Israelite identity is a continuation of Canaanite traditions that were repackaged into the chosen people's narrative. For example, the name Yahweh comes from the Canaanite pantheon, and El, a general term referring to deities, can be tied to a god with the same name. Therefore, when the Bible is studied historically, and the aspect of divine revelation is minimized, you'll find that the overarching story is completely transformed. Instead of the Canaanites or Western Semites being framed as villainous, they are the progenitors of the Israelite culture.

When you get to the New Testament, another evolution of the Israelite identity emerges. The best way to think about the New Testament doctrines is open-sourcing of the Israelite faith. No longer is the inheritance of the Kingdom of God focused on birthright, but now readers are introduced to the concept of adoption into the Kingdom through Jesus Christ's sacrifice. This open-sourced approach to religion radically shifted the tribal and nationalistic ties of how faith was understood for centuries. Now, Gentiles were also allowed into the Kingdom through adoption. Where Israel was once thought of as the son of God, the Christian framework now places Jesus in that position, creating salvation through Christ as the truth.

Biblical Timelines

History continuously evolves, and because the Bible is a living tradition, the story has not yet completely unfolded. Even though the Bible was canonized by the third century, understanding of the text is continuously changing. Religious movements like the protestant reformation, later developments in the New World, and today, where texts are constantly interpreted through contemporary lenses, means the story is continuously evolving. Therefore, you need to think of Biblical history as alive and dynamic.

However, if the focus is placed on the writing, compiling, and canonizing of the Bible, then the historical timeline can be divided into seven key periods.

Late Bronze Age

This era of Bible tradition development can be considered as the age when the foundations of religion and traditions were laid. The Late Bronze Age spanned between 1550 BC and 1200 BC. The Ugarit – in northern Syria – was a bustling cosmopolitan city where many diverse religious and cultural practices were embraced, some of which evolved into Israelite customs and law. Deities such as Asherah, Baal, and El were worshiped in that region. All three are mentioned by name in the Bible, and one of them, El or Elohim, references the God of the Israelites.

During Pharoah Merneptah's reign, Israel is mentioned in the Merneptah stela (an inscription by Merneptah, a pharaoh in ancient Egypt who reigned from 1213 to 1203 BCE), which ties to the Exodus narrative of Israelite slaves in Egypt. The stela boasts victories over various Canaanite groups, including Israel, ending with the statement, "Everyone who is restless, he has been bound." It is still arguable that the Biblical Exodus under the prophet Moses was a literal event because of a lack of archeological evidence of millions of people camping in the Sinai desert. However, the Exodus account may have been a true but exaggerated occurrence.

Iron I Period

The first Iron Age was when the Israelite identity had been firmly crafted, and you can begin to see texts emerging. Some sayings in Genesis and poems in Judges 5 originate from this period. This era of the Israelite nation was predynastic, with loosely cooperating tribes claiming Israelite identity. Archeology from this period discovered inscriptions on metal items like arrowheads, including names and burial verses. Near the end of the Iron Age I, Israel got its first king, Saul, who would precede the famous and legendary King David.

Iron II Period

This period in Israelite history is when the nation emerged as a powerful force in the region. The rule of King David and his treaty with Tyre established Israel as a hegemony over neighboring cultures. Following King David, the famous King Solomon established trade and diplomatic relations with Egypt, and the Jerusalem temple was built.

When King Solomon died, Israel was thrown into turmoil, resulting in a split into the Northern Kingdom of Israel and the Southern Kingdom of Judah. Jeroboam I became the first king in the North. The Gezer calendar inscription was created between 900 BC and 800 BC, one of the earliest sources of written Hebrew. Sections of Psalms and portions of 2 Samuel may trace the origins back to this period. It is theorized that parts of the Old Testament come from the compilation of two source texts: the J source (which uses the name *Yahweh* and was later translated into Jehovah) and the E source (using the name *El* or *Elohim*). The J source may have originated from the Southern Kingdom around 900 to 800 BC.

Between 882 and 871 BC, Omri established the capital of the Northern Kingdom in Samaria. Later, King Ahab created a coalition with Tyre, which was solidified by his marriage to the infamous Jezebel. During this time, many of the Bible's most prominent prophets emerged, such as Elijah, Elisha, Isaiah, and Hosea. In the second Iron Age, the bulk of Deuteronomy was written. Hoshea, the last king of Israel, acted as a vassal for the Assyrian Empire. Many Old Testament writings were likely circulating in the Second Iron Age, including the Psalms, Proverbs, and First and Second Kings. The Israelites entered the Babylonian captivity with the fall of Jerusalem and the destruction of the temple.

Persian Period

In this period, Judah became a province of the Persian Empire. Under the rule of Cyrus, the Israelites were allowed to return to their homeland. An initial group of Judaens, led by the governor Sheshbazzar, returned to Judah. The next governor of the Persian province of Judah was Zerubbabel. He rebuilt the Temple of Jerusalem, but it was not as prestigious as the first. In collaboration with the religious leader Jeshua, under the inspiration of the prophecy of Haggai, they undertook this project to restore the dignity of Israel. Following the reconstruction of the temple, Nehemiah rebuilt the walls of Jerusalem. The books of Daniel, Esther, Chronicles, Song of Songs, and the priestly compilation of Psalms were completed between 300 BC and 400 BC. You also find that Job, in its modern form, may have been completed at this time.

Hellenistic Period

The Hellenistic Period of Biblical history spans from 333 BC to 165 BC, beginning when Alexander the Great conquered Egypt and the Levant. The establishment of the Samaritan priestly order began due to conflicts within the priesthood. Once Alexander died, his kingdom was split between his generals, including Ptolemaic Egypt and the Seleucids in Syria. By the mid-200s, the earliest Dead Sea Scrolls were written, and the Greek Septuagint translation of the Bible was written. Judea revolted against the Seleucids, who ushered in the Maccabean monarchy. By the end of the Hellenistic period, many Old Testament scriptures were distributed widely, and the Torah and the prophetic writings were considered authoritative.

Maccabean Monarchy

The Maccabean monarchy started with the defeat of the Seleucids, who had dedicated the temple in Jerusalem to Zeus. Once their armies were defeated, the temple was restored, instituting Judas Maccabeus's rule over Judea. The restoration of the temple is celebrated in the book 1 Maccabees. Following the rule of Judas, his brother Johnathon took over and fought the Nabateans, prompting the fortification of Jerusalem. In this era, conflicts within the priesthood resulted in the development of multiple communities, one of which was the Dead Sea Scroll Movement.

Roman Period

This is probably the most popular period in the mainstream consciousness because it was the era in which Jesus Christ was born. Since Christianity is the most practiced faith in the world today, it makes sense that this era would be primarily focused on it. The Roman period significantly impacted the modern Jewish religion because this was when the Talmudic writings were completed. The New Testament books were compiled around the years 50 to 100 AD based on oral traditions passed around by the growing Christian religion. In 70 AD, the Romans destroyed the Jerusalem temple. Eventually, the Romans embraced Christianity as the state religion after years of persecuting the Christians, which helped spread the faith to become as widely practiced as it is today.

Timeline Activity

In the space below, draw a timeline of the key periods of Biblical History. Highlight important events and explain how they link to what is contained in the Bible narrative.

Geopolitics and the Israelite Identity

Many tribes inhabited the ancient Near East, which resulted in a plurality of spiritual beliefs. As it was a trade route, nomadic tribes would cross the area, contributing to the local systems. Adding to this mixing pot, conquest and conflict within the Near East fundamentally shaped how religion would be understood. Examining the Biblical text, you find influences from these various groups. For example, the New Testament was written predominantly in Greek due to the Hellenistic contribution to Judaic culture at the time.

Exploration of the Bible requires knowing that it occurred in different areas and times throughout the Middle East. The influence of Assyrians, Egyptians, Hittites, and Edomites is clear when the text is understood as having emerged in a particular context. Some even cite ancient Egypt as influencing the Bible through resurrection narratives and rising gods and as one of the earliest forms of monotheism under the Akhenaten rule. However, instead of one culture feeding into another, a more accurate view would be that the intermixing in the area facilitated the emergence and spreading of similar ideas. For example, the Persian Zoroastrianism religion may have influenced Jewish ideas of an adversarial force personified as Satan and the positive of God existing in a battle.

Within the Israelite traditions, there was a diversity of thought. Part of the reason that the Jewish religious establishment was against the emergence of Jesus as a Messianic figure was the disastrous impacts similar thoughts had had in the past. Jewish opinions at the time were split between two major schools: the teachers who focused on the law and the messianic schools that prophesied a coming messiah that would free them from Roman rule. Jesus was not the first or only messianic figure to emerge in rebellion against the Romans. More violent messiah prototypes who led rebellions and the masses of people who followed them were quickly dealt with and killed by Roman soldiers. The priestly and leadership class of Judah noticed this repeating cycle, so the establishment pushed to move away from apocalyptic interpretations of texts for self-preservation. Hence, they may have had problems with Jesus, one in a long line of Messiahs taking on this archetype.

Through the window of understanding internal Jewish conflicts, disagreements between tribes inhabiting the same area, and the numerous conflicts that occurred, many of the Bible's laws, teachings, and interpretations begin to make sense. Besides the geopolitics of literature, there is also the element of divine revelation that deals with fulfilled prophecy and the supernatural realm. Many scholars refrain from this supernatural aspect of the Bible because there is no way to prove or study it. However, if you consider divine revelation to be true, it can reframe the meaning of the Bible and further contribute to the book's geopolitical formation because the decisions of believers are generally driven by their faith and how they interpret their beliefs. The strong belief of martyrs who died for Christianity in its earliest days is why it spread so far. People were in awe of the conviction early believers demonstrated, so they were enticed to join the faith that believers were willing to die for. Therefore, the interplay between faith, politics, and history makes the Bible one of the most captivating textual compilations to ever exist.

The Bible and Critical Thinking

Christianity, Judaism, and the modern understanding of the Bible could have looked entirely different had a few key moments panned out differently. Therefore, critical thinking in the Biblical sense requires minimizing biases and reviewing all the information available in order to draw conclusions about the text. Studying the Bible takes a lifetime of dedication. There are numerous translations and theological understandings of the text, so you will find many Christian denominations and Jewish schools of thought with conflicting ideas, even though leaders have dedicated innumerable hours to seeking the truth of the Bible.

New ways of interpreting the text are emerging with movements like progressive Christianity that highlight the social justice aspects of the Gospel and aim to make Christianity more inclusive for various groups like the LGBT community. In the modern age, much information is emerging, and data travels so quickly that you can reach it immediately. Moreover, you have more access to information than many of the Biblical scholars and enthusiasts of the past would have had. It means that critical thinking is more important now than ever because of the influx of information and the flood of conflicting views.

The crux of critical thinking is adjusting to new information instead of remaining firm and immovable.[58]

The crux of critical thinking is adjusting to new information instead of remaining firm and immovable. Being open-minded to new information and analyzing it according to the latest research gives you the foundational principle to a fuller understanding of the Bible. Considering factors like translations, politics, history, and the theological interpretation of the text gives you a well-rounded view. With open-minded study, you can inch closer to a complete view of this ancient compilation of books that have so profoundly shaped the world.

As you continue through these chapters, you will gain more information about the Bible and be taught to think critically and question the narratives placed before you so that you can assess the details with a fine-toothed comb and unearth the hidden gems.

How do you currently understand the Bible?

_____

_____

_____

_____

What influenced that view?

_____

_____

_____

_____

Are you open to having those views challenged? Why, or why not?

_____

_____

_____

_____

Research Activity

Research the differences that emerge when a person accepts divine revelation to interpret the Biblical text and when a person rejects supernatural interventions.

How can you understand the development of the ancient Israelite religion and later Christianity through the interpretation of divine revelation?

How can you understand the development of the Israelite religion and Christianity if divine revelation is rejected?

What are the possible geopolitical and historical reasons that the Torah, or Pentateuch, was written and compiled as it is known in modern times?

What geopolitical and historical reasons resulted in the transition from the oral traditions of the early followers of Christ to seeing the Gospels codified into standardized scripture?

Section 2: Genesis to Deuteronomy: The First 5 Books

The Bible's first five books, the Torah or the Pentateuch, are foundational to the text's narrative structure. The beauty of scripture is that it has been written from different authors' viewpoints in varying cultural contexts over hundreds of years, yet an overarching narrative has emerged. The structures and moral lessons of the Bible's first five books continue to echo and unfold as the story progresses.

In this Chapter, you will dive into the thematic elements of the Torah and examine how you can apply these lessons today. From the formation of modern law and how civilization is shaped by personal experiences, the Torah is an incredible mirror to hold up in

The Bible's first five books, the Torah or the Pentateuch, are foundational to the text's narrative structure.[89]

order to reflect on your life and society. The Pentateuch is arguably the most essential part of the Bible because the stories that follow are built onto the themes already revealed through its powerful narratives. You explore God's relationship with humankind and, by extension, their interactions with each other to reveal miraculous stories of judgment, mercy, redemption, and salvation from Genesis to Deuteronomy. The timeless stories and principles they reveal are still as relevant as they ever were, so their exploration can unpack a lot about yourself and how your life can embody some of the highest principles of truth.

Plotting Key Narratives from Genesis to Deuteronomy

The central plot that runs through the Bible's first five books, or the Torah, the Hebrew word for law, is God's tumultuous relationship with mankind. The Israelite God is a radical reframing of how the ancient world understood deities. Although many of the same practices and agreements were required by the God of the Bible and other gods, the central difference is love. The vital focal point in the Torah is that although God gets angry and curses His people, a fatherly relationship is maintained throughout the constant struggle between obedience and rebellion.

Genesis

The word *Genesis* can be translated as the beginning. Genesis focuses on the start of the cosmos and sets the stage for the beginning of God's relationship with humankind. The cosmos begins as this chaotic and inhabitable place, or as the Bible calls it, "formless and void." Then God orders it, creating a world that He constantly refers to as "good." The Bible introduces the first humans, Adam and Eve. Some interpret them as literal people, while others take the story more symbolically. Either way, there is meaning embedded into their names. Adam means "Humanity," and Eve means "Life." In this way, these two characters were the first representatives of what humanity's relationship with God would look like.

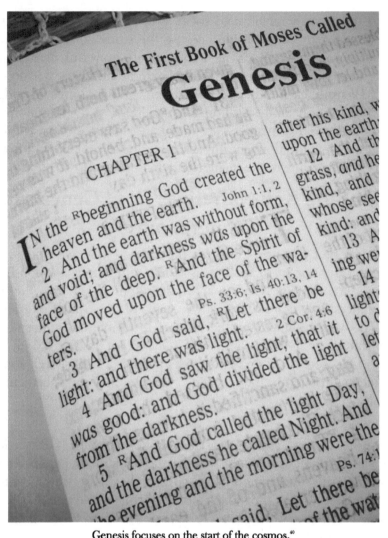

The First Book of Moses Called

Genesis

CHAPTER 1

IN the ᴿbeginning God created the heaven and the earth.   John 1:1, 2

2 And the earth was without form, and void; and darkness was upon the face of the deep. ᴿAnd the Spirit of God moved upon the face of the wa-ters.   Ps. 33:6; Is. 40:13, 14

3 And God said, ᴿLet there be light: and there was light.   2 Cor. 4:6

4 And God saw the light, that it was good: and God divided the light from the darkness.

5 ᴿAnd God called the light Day, and the darkness he called Night. And the evening and the morning were the   Ps. 74:1

...said, Let there be

after his kind, w upon the earth:
12 And th grass, and he kind, and whose see kind: and
13 A ing we
14 light to c let a

Genesis focuses on the start of the cosmos.⁴⁰

Adam and Eve had not yet received the law, which would come later with the prophet Moses. However, they were given a rule not to eat the fruit from the Tree of Knowledge of Good and Evil. When they ate the fruit, it represented a departure from following the desires of God to humanity relying on their understanding, which inevitably came with devastating consequences.

The theme of humans following their desires against what God has asked them to do is repeated throughout the Torah, especially in the first Book of Genesis. You get the first murder where Cain killed Abel. Then Lamech, his descendent, brags that his wickedness is even greater, eventually leading to the tower of Babel, where humanity attempts to build a structure to reach the heavens. Now, the theme of humankind following their whims gets fleshed out a little more because, instead of following God's guidelines to get closer to Him on His terms, they attempted to achieve it through their own struggles. God knows this will not end well because impure humans cannot get close to Him without dying, so He shows them mercy by confusing their languages and splitting them into nations. Each nation has its god at this time, but through His relationship with Abraham, the God of Israel reveals that he is greater than them, which will become more significant later in the narrative in Exodus.

Before Abraham, you get Noah, who built the ark before God flooded the Earth. After generations of wickedness, God finally got fed up and decided to end the world. Noah and his family members enter the ark as the world is flooded. This is one of the most striking depictions of God's justice and mercy because He does not destroy everyone but gives a few faithful individuals a chance. The next major player in the Biblical narrative was Abraham, through whom God established the covenantal system. God made three major promises to Abraham. First, he would have many descendants. Secondly, he would get land for his people and, lastly, all nations would be blessed through his seed.

An interpretation of Noah's ark.[41]

Abraham's son Jacob received his birthright, and he had twelve sons. His favorite son was Joseph. Jacob gave Joseph a colorful coat, which made his brothers jealous. They plotted to murder him but ended up selling him into slavery. With the gifts God gave Joseph, he rose through the ranks and became one of Egypt's most powerful people. Famine struck many nations in the Middle East, which led Joseph's brothers to seek refuge in Egypt. They arrived in Egypt to find their brother held a high position and could help them. He remarked on how their plans for wickedness, God, had turned into plans for prosperity. This was the instant when the transmutation aspect of the Torah, and by extension, the Bible, was initially revealed because God's all-knowing might could transform evil into righteousness even when it seemed hopeless.

Exodus

Some generations after Joseph, the Israelites were enslaved in Egypt by a wicked pharaoh. The Exodus narrative of God delivering the Israelites out of captivity under the leadership of Moses began. Pharoah refused to free the Israelites, which brought plagues to Egypt. Through these terrifying plagues, justice was emphasized. For example, the final plague was killing the Egyptians' firstborn sons, just like the pharaoh commanded the murder of the eldest sons of Israel. The Israelites had to slaughter a Passover lamb and rub the blood on their doors to avoid their firstborns being killed. Blood in the Bible represents life, so this symbolizes that only life could enter the doors of the Israelites. This is linked to the later part of the Torah (in Deuteronomy), when Moses urged the Israelites to choose life.

The Exodus provides the narrative of God delivering the Israelites out of captivity.[42]

There was the concept of suzerain and vassal kings in the ancient world. Vassal kings were ruled by suzerain kings from larger nations or empires. To keep the peace, they would make agreements called covenants. These covenants typically shared certain elements. Firstly, they emphasized the generosity of the suzerain king, who helped the nation of the vassal to defeat another enemy or by allowing them to live in a certain way. Next, they included curses, which were the consequences that would occur if the vassal king broke the agreement. Also included were blessings, which were the privileges the vassal king would enjoy under the suzerain rule. Lastly, there were remembrance rituals to reinforce the contract, usually done under the names or traditions of the gods of both kingdoms. This system was mirrored in the covenant system God set up with Israel after they escaped from Egypt, which is further explored in the Book of Leviticus.

Leviticus

The Levitical narrative shows the restoration of God's relationship with the people of Israel. If you trace the story back to the beginning, God dwelled among humans until the fall of Adam and Eve, caused by their disobedience. In Leviticus, God is coming full circle to dwell among the children of Israel. He commands the construction of a Tabernacle, which is like a tent temple in the middle of the desert. Once the Tabernacle was built, God dwelled within it to guide Israel.

However, Moses could not enter the Tabernacle, and the priests who went into it inappropriately died, which resulted in the institution of laws and protocols to ensure purity. Firstly, dietary laws were instituted stating what could be eaten and what could not. Secondly, states of purity were instituted according to illnesses and bodily fluids. Then, moral laws pertaining to relationships, sex, and justice were introduced. The priestly class had an even higher standard to maintain because they were the representatives of the community who stood before the Lord. These laws set a standard of what it took to remain close to God.

Most efforts are communal and focused on a relationship with the Lord, and it was noted that the concepts of clean and unclean were not necessarily the same as right and wrong. It was more about God and holding a high standard of holiness to enter His presence or to be closer to him. This thematically emphasized that a perfect God sees it fit to love people and make ways to reach out and connect with them. God began taking on a character of humility, which would later be highlighted in the narrative of Christ's sacrifice, but this was where the story began.

Numbers

The Book of Numbers focuses on the Israelite's time in the wilderness or the desert. The journey, which should have taken a couple of weeks, was extended to forty years. On the way to the Promised Land, the Israelites spent time in three main sections of the desert, namely, Mount Sinai, Paran, and Moab, on the edge of the Promised Land. Living in God's presence was started in the previous Book of Leviticus but is continued in Numbers. The Israelite camp and their traveling formation were set up with a specific emphasis on God's order and the structure of purity. When camping, the Tabernacle was in the center, surrounded by the priestly Levite tribes with the other tribes surrounding them. The Ark of the Covenant, containing God's presence, was carried in the front during travel, followed by the Levites, Judah, and the rest of the tribes. The symbolic significance of God being in the center while camping and in the front while traveling was to demonstrate that He would always be the guide.

During their travels, God always made provision for the Israelites through water, manna, and fowl so they could have meat to eat. However, despite the blessings, the Israelites always complained, stating they had enjoyed a better standard of life under the oppression of Egypt. When the cloud of God's presence moved, the Israelites were commanded to follow. Throughout their desert trek, the Israelites constantly went against their agreement with God, resulting in multiple curses, including getting attacked by snakes. How the Israelites healed from snake bites is an interesting story. A bronze snake was placed on a stake, and whenever anyone was attacked, the victim was told to look at it in order to heal. This symbolizes turning to God for your needs, and in the Christian narrative, is considered an early depiction of how Christ would be nailed to a cross for the sins of mankind.

One of the most pertinent curses was that "a generation would have to pass before they got into the Promised Land," which is why the desert journey was extended for so long. This is how the theme of balance between free will and God's will was introduced. According to the story, God wanted His people to follow Him and dwell in His presence so that He could reward them. However, God did not force this outcome. Therefore, at every step, there was a choice to reject the fellowship of God, but there would be consequences.

The theme of God transmuting evil to good was repeated in the region of Moab. As the Israelites passed through Moab to the Promised Land, the King was understandably concerned because this large nation was traveling through his territory. King Balak's concern prompted him to employ a powerful sorcerer, Balaam. Balaam recognized the unmistakable power of the God of Israel, so he prayed to Him so that he could curse the Israelites. However, Balaam found that he could only voice blessings every time he tried to curse them. The final blessing Balaam uttered was that God's promise to Abraham to bless his descendants and establish a nation would come through the leadership of a mighty Israelite king. This links the narrative back to Genesis, showing that this is one story instead of an isolated book or chapter. The transmutation of the "evil to good" theme emerged in that while the Israelites were rebelling in the valley, God was still blessing them at the top of the mountain.

Deuteronomy

The Book of Deuteronomy covers Moses's final address to the people of Israel before he died and handed over leadership to Joshua. Moses would never enter the Promised Land but brought Israel right to the edge of it. In this epic speech, Moses outlined everything Israel needed to pay attention to as they entered the Promised Land.

The Book of Deuteronomy covers Moses's final address to the people of Israel before he died and handed over leadership to Joshua.[43]

Moses opened the speech by highlighting their constant rebellion. He then transitioned into encouraging the new generation that will enter the land to not be like their ancestors but to obey God diligently. Moses reminded them about the laws of the covenant they made with God, expanding on them to make them relevant to a new generation.

One of the key revelations in Deuteronomy is the Shema, a declaration Jewish people still make today in prayer twice a day. The Shema is in Deuteronomy 6:4-5 which states, "Hear, O Israel: The Lord our God, the Lord is one. Love the Lord your God with all your heart and with all your soul and with all your strength." This is the crux of the message Moses left the Nation before his departure. Moses had to emphasize that the God of Israel is one because as they entered the Promised Land, they would dwell among a multitude of nations worshiping diverse gods. He made another statement, later echoed in the New Testament, outlining that Israel had a choice to obey and love God or rebel. Moses warned that Israel could choose death or life and continued to encourage the nation to choose life. This choice of life is a call back to the blood of the Passover lamb that freed them from Egypt.

Moses predicted that the Israelites would rebel, causing them to be exiled from the land. He concluded that this is because their hearts were hardened with selfishness and a desire to follow their own will instead of that of the Lord. To highlight that a flesh struggle is uniquely human and is deeply ingrained into the genetics of humanity, Moses linked this hardening of the heart back to the Genesis narrative when Adam and Eve fell in the Garden of Eden. However, he ended with a message of hope that the Lord would make a way to soften their hearts, which again elevated the theme of the transmutation of negative into positive. It laid the foundation for the story of Christ as a savior because, from the Christian understanding, His sacrifice opened the path for humankind to receive new hearts.

Writing Activity

Plot a visual representation of the major stories of the Torah. Explain the lessons that emerge from each story and highlight how they each link to form a grander narrative.

Themes and Moral Lessons of the Torah

Thematically, the Torah reveals a few major principles. The hearts of humanity are turned to pursue wickedness. People need to work toward addressing this issue of having evil hearts by following God's commands, including rituals, laws, and festivals of remembrance. God is perfect. So, the purer you are, the closer you can get to His unfiltered presence. Although there are laws to obtain the purity that allows you to have fellowship with God, He understands that people will fall short, so he continuously shows humanity mercy throughout the narrative.

In this way, the Torah sets up the theme of humanity's constant struggle against their desires so that they can meet God's standard. Unlike teachings that promote finding yourself, the Bible is radically different. The Torah sets up the story that humanity is required to deny themselves alignment with God's desires. Suppose God is viewed as the personification of the highest good or the most righteous principles humankind can pursue. In that case, the central message of the Torah is to diminish your personal lust for a higher purpose or the spiritual mission of following God.

The communal is emphasized over the personal. Therefore, the purest people, or the priesthood, go before God to represent humanity. On the Day of Atonement, as outlined in Leviticus, a sacrifice is made where a goat is slaughtered as an offering to God, and another is set free into the wilderness carrying the sins of the community. This emphasis on forgiveness balances the justice and purity of the strict laws. Through this window of atonement, God's mercy is brought into memory to emphasize how people should engage with each other in the spirit of understanding and forgiveness. So, in addition to striving for purity in the letter of the law, love and mercy are in the heart of the Torah.

Post-Reading Activity

What lessons have you learned from each of the books of the Torah? How can some of the principles be applied in your life today?

Reflections on the Laws of the Torah and Their Modern Significance

Some laws from the Torah are known as natural laws. These emerge from cultures all over the world because they are necessary for civilization or society to sustain itself. Natural laws include principles like not lying, stealing, or murdering. In addition to these natural or moral laws, the Torah has purity laws, which are slightly different. As God descended to dwell in proximity to His people, they needed to purify themselves, which meant that some practices or conditions were considered clean or unclean.

The central message of the Torah that still rings true in the modern world is that the hearts of humanity lead them astray: Reflect on every selfish decision you or that people have made that resulted in negative outcomes. As much as people preach kindness, love, unity, forgiveness, and patience, these values seldom express themselves. A constant internal struggle aligns with these higher values against the instant gratification or easier path of selfish desires. The festivals and rituals established in the Torah bring out remembrance of God, which reminds people of the path they should walk.

Struggles and Triumphs of Biblical Characters and How They Relate to You

Throughout the Torah, you see humanity battling against their desires to follow God's ways. When the characters submit to God, they are blessed even when their backs are against the wall. When the characters rebel and turn away from God's instructions, they are cursed, bringing further hardship into their lives, but God makes a way for them to return to Him. Linked to the messages from God on curses and blessings, your obedience is always accompanied by Him, allowing you to make free choices. Still, because of His perfectly just nature, people must live with the consequences of their decisions.

When the characters submit to God, they are blessed even when their backs are against the wall."

Which of the characters in the Torah do you relate to most and why?

_____
_____
_____
_____
_____
_____
_____
_____
_____
_____
_____

How can you map their triumphs and struggles and relate them to your life? What value can you extract from your understanding?

_____
_____
_____
_____
_____
_____
_____
_____
_____
_____
_____
_____

The Shift from Scholarly to Transformative

Studying the Torah through a scholarly lens is admirable, but, in essence, these books are meant to be applied and not merely studied. Whether you are a believer or not, much wisdom can be gained from embracing the eternal truths outlined in these scriptures. Memorizing verses in the Torah and understanding the historical background can be enlightening and an excellent way to expand your knowledge. However, when the spiritual and philosophical aspects of the book are applied, only then is the scripture truly transformative. The two core messages of the Torah are that God can use your wickedness and transform it into goodness, and if you suppress your selfish desires and follow God for a higher purpose, only then will you be blessed.

How do you think you can apply some of the central themes of the Torah to transform your life?

_____

_____

_____

_____

_____

_____

_____

_____

_____

_____

_____

_____

Section 3: Books from the Old Testament

Now that you have explored the Bible's first five books, you are ready to delve into the Old Testament as a whole. This section will predominantly provide an overview of the Hebrew Bible and set the stage for more in-depth research in the subsequent sections. After studying these theoretical explanations and completing the activities, you will know how to analyze the Old Testament's literary styles and identify the major themes from the text.

The Old Testament was originally written in Hebrew.⁴⁵

Historical and Cultural Context of the Old Testament

The Hebrew Bible, the Tanakh, is split into three sections: the Torah, Nevi'im, and Ketuvim. The Torah or Pentateuch has been explored in the previous section. The Torah is the first five books of the Old Testament that deliver the law. The Nevi'im are the books of the prophets, and the Ketuvim can be translated as the writings. This three-part division of scripture is ancient and comes from when the texts were still recorded in scrolls. The ancient Israelites were likely to have understood the text in this way because there is a logical flow when organized like this. Furthermore, modern Jewish people who read the scriptures in the original Hebrew still use this method to divide the Old Testament.

A more contemporary division of the Old Testament groups the scriptures into categories of historical books, poetic or wisdom books, and prophetic books. The historical books encompass the Torah, Joshua, Judges, Ruth, 1 & 2 Samuel, 1 & 2 Kings, and 1 & 2 Chronicles. The poetic books are Proverbs, Psalms, Job, Song of Solomon, and Ecclesiastes. The rest of the Old Testament falls under prophetic writings, including Ezekiel, Jeremiah, Amos, and Hosea.

The Torah's themes continue throughout the rest of the Old Testament. The overarching narrative that is unveiled as the story progresses is God's relationship of love, mercy, and judgment for a people who consistently rebelled against him. The prophetic writing in the Book of Hosea encompasses this relationship well because it is compared to an adulterous marriage. Hosea was married to Gomer, a woman who continuously had extramarital affairs. According to the Torah's laws, Hosea had every right to divorce her. Instead of God telling him to abandon Gomer for her shortcomings, he tells Hosea to take her back and show her compassion, a metaphor for God's relationship with Israel. Although God is justified in abandoning his people for their worship or idols, he returns to them in His love and mercy.

It would be too extensive for scribes to write the details of every person in Israel's life, so the focus falls on three main groups – judges, kings, and prophets. When Joshua led Israel into the Promised Land, they still followed God's laws. Once Joshua died, Israel was led by a succession of judges, and the nation deteriorated once again after the Mosaic period in the wilderness. The judges of Israel were not like those you would think of in a court system. They could be more closely related to tribal chiefs. The prophets acted as the mouthpiece of God and, at different periods, revealed blessings for Israel or curses against them. However, they often concluded with a message of hope for the future as God left open a pathway for restoration and redemption.

As Israelites dwelt among the Canaanites, they worshiped the foreign gods. They tumbled down these rebellious rabbit holes so much that they became precisely like the Canaanites, so God elected to drive them out of the land. They were immoral and even practiced child sacrifice. So, God used the surrounding nations to judge Israel, eventually leading to exile from the Promised Land. Through many tumultuous occurrences, the Israelites were exiled to Babylon. The Old Testament concludes with a story of hope for the coming Messiah and the reconstruction of the temple.

Activity 1

Highlight five stories in the Old Testament where God's presence left the Israelites.

_____

_____

_____

_____

_____

_____

_____

_____

_____

_____

_____

_____

_____

_____

_____

Explain why God's presence left and what had to be done to get back in alignment with God's will.

_____

_____

_____

_____

_____

_____

_____

_____

_____

_____

_____

_____

Highlight five stories in the Old Testament where God blessed the Israelites.

_____

_____

_____

_____

_____

_____

_____

_____

_____

_____

_____

_____

_____

Explain how these blessings link to the theme of God's mercy and redemption and God using wickedness to transform into righteousness.

The History Books

These 17 books tell the story of humanity and Israel from creation until the fall of the Northern and Southern kingdoms. The narrative starts by showing how Israel is redeemed and saved from enslavement under the brutal rule of the pharaoh. They trace their journey through the wilderness into the Promised Land. The books detail the period of Judges, where Israel rapidly deteriorated and became like the pagan nations they replaced. Israel transitions from the period of judges into the time of kings. Internal conflicts caused the kingdom to split into northern Israel and Judah in the south. The history books of Israel conclude with the fall of both kingdoms and Israel's entry into a new captivity.

Thematic Exploration of the Old Testament through King David

The life of King David perfectly encapsulates how God blesses you when you follow his laws and how he curses you when you depart from them. It fully captures how there is always room for redemption and repentance no matter how far you have fallen and how evil can be used to ultimately facilitate righteous outcomes.

David is one of the most famous kings in the Bible, and he is rivaled only by his son, Solomon. King David's first act of heroism was defeating Goliath, a Philistine warrior everyone feared. The shepherd boy was accustomed to killing bears and wolves in the fields, so he used his skills with a slingshot to defeat the giant.

King Saul was the first ruler of Israel, but his wickedness overcame him. As David grew in popularity, King Saul became jealous and fearful, thinking David would overthrow his throne. Saul tried to kill David but failed. Through their rivalry, David's character is revealed, as he spares Saul's life continuously, even when he has easy opportunities to kill him.

David eventually ascends to the throne. He was a righteous king but also fell short. He lusted after Bathsheba, who was a married woman, entering an adulterous relationship with her. He sent Bathsheba's husband, Uriah, to the frontline of a battle to die so that he could marry her. King David succeeded in his plan, and God was disappointed in him. Nathan called out David for his wickedness, and, as judgment, the son he conceived with Bathsheba died.

Under David, the kingdom of Israel was strengthened and solidified. He wanted to build a temple for the Lord but did not achieve this goal. However, King Solomon, his son, built the

A statue of King David, playing the harp.[46]

temple David had dreamed of. Through David's line, Jesus Christ, the redeemer of Israel, was born. However, many kings who ruled after David – including Solomon – descended into wickedness and idolatry.

Activity 2

Construct a storyboard of the life of King David, noting the high and low points and the consequences. As you create this visual representation, reflect on the themes of God's justice, mercy, and duality, which exist in the heart of mankind. Include parallels to your life in your storyboard as a way to mediate deeply on the wisdom of this historical account.

_____

_____

_____

_____

_____

_____

_____

_____

_____

_____

_____

_____

The Wisdom Books

The three main wisdom books are Job, Ecclesiastes, and Proverbs. Some people include Psalms in the wisdom traditions, but the entire book does not fully match the parameters to fit into this category. The wisdom tradition opens with the Book of Proverbs. Typically, proverbs can be understood as short sayings that communicate lessons within specific cultures or groups. The Book of Proverbs contains lessons but also a narrative structure. The first part of Proverbs is presented as a father speaking to a son and guiding him. In the later part of the text, wisdom is personified as a woman and can be related to a motherly figure.

Proverbs teaches how to be wise, which in the Israelite context is not only about gaining knowledge but encompasses what you can practically apply. So, Proverbs teaches you how to live well, beginning with the fear of God so that you keep his commandments. Unlike the Mosaic law or the covenants, Proverbs makes no promises but functions with probability insofar that if you make wise decisions, positive outcomes will likely result.

Ecclesiastes throws a wrench into the mechanics of Proverbs. Although the author acknowledges it is good to live with wisdom and the fear of God, they highlight that there is no guarantee you will live well. They make this point by expressing that bad people often live great and prosperous lives, and good people often suffer. The Hebrew word encapsulating Ecclesiastes theme is *"hevel."* Hevel is written as "meaningless" in many English translations, but a more direct translation is vapor or smoke. When you consider the qualities of smoke, you see how it maps to life.

Everything is temporary or elusive. The author of Ecclesiastes emphasizes this through the concepts of time and death. On a long enough timeline, all your achievements are meaningless. Most people have been long forgotten. On a cosmic scale, the entire existence of humanity is less than a blink. Therefore, everything you value will disappear like smoke in the wind. Death is used to illustrate the same point. Everyone meets the same end, whether wise, foolish, rich, or poor. Death is the equalizer no one can avoid. Hence, this short life on the planet is like smoke; people try to grab it, but it slips through their fingers. This seems grim, but the author concludes that the meaning of life exists in accepting this changing, paradoxical, and fleeting nature of life.

The Book of Job explores one of the most difficult questions anyone can ask. Why do bad things happen to good people? The story of Job opens with a court in heaven, where God points to Job as an example of righteousness. Satan argues that Job is only righteous because God rewards him, and if he were to remove his hedge of protection from Job, he would surely curse God. As Job falls into suffering, the theme of justice is explored through his conversations with his friends and God. Job confesses his innocence and cries out to God to explain why all this suffering has suddenly happened to him. His friends say Job must have brought this suffering on himself because God is truly just. However, the court in heaven reveals that Job was blameless, so this cannot be the answer.

The book does not reveal why bad things happen to good people but puts humanity's place in the cosmos into perspective. God reveals to Job that complicated structures hold the universe together, and his finite mind could not possibly understand it. Therefore, Job is not able to question God's justice. The answer God provides about why good things happen to bad people is that it is far too complicated for a human to comprehend. Job humbles himself and repents in this realization, and God gifts him back everything he lost. This ties into Ecclesiastes insofar as people must accept what they cannot control or explain. When the wisdom books are viewed through the lens of the extended Old Testament theme of the cycle of justice, curses, and redemption, they reveal that it is not as simple as mere surface-level analysis, so trusting in God is vital.

Activity 3

Consider the Proverb's central message to live well according to scriptural principles. Consider Job's message to humble yourself before God. Now, reflect on the wisdom of Ecclesiastes to let go of control and accept what God gives you.

How can you apply these themes to your life as it currently stands?

_____

_____

_____

_____

_____

_____

_____

_____

_____

_____

_____

Prophetic Writings

One central message is delivered to Israel by every prophet, even though the specifics of their lives teach unique lessons. Every prophet delivered the message that God should be worshipped – *and God alone* – in order to be blessed.

Or you can rebel and face God's judgment.

Israel's history reflects this message as they prospered and fell. The prophets always followed the same structure in their writings. First, they called out the sins of the people. Then, they asked the people to return to God's laws. Lastly, they warned the people of the judgment they would suffer in the event of their rebellion.

One of the more unique prophets was Jonah because he was controversial. The Book of Jonah ends on a cliffhanger with God asking a question that Jonah does not answer. Jonah's character is already in question because he prophesied that a wicked king, Jeroboam II, would succeed and gain territory. At the same time, Amos, another prophet of God, gave the opposite message, saying the king would lose it all due to his wickedness.

The Book of Jonah sets up the extension of salvation to the gentile nations and encapsulates the Old Testament theme of the transformation of evil into good. Jonah was an Israelite and of God's people. However, he disobeyed God, and the pagans he met obeyed God. God sent Jonah to the Ninevites to tell them their city would be overturned. However, Jonah fled in the opposite direction, ending up on a pagan boat. When a storm approached, Jonah was thrown overboard, and the pagans repented and worshiped God, highlighting the transformation of Jonah's wickedness into the positive outcome of winning souls to worship the true God. Jonah was swallowed by a whale, and God allowed him to follow through with his mission. Jonah reluctantly delivered the prophecy to the Ninevites. Jonah fled not out of fear but because he hated the Ninevites and wanted them destroyed.

Jonah was swallowed by a whale, and God allowed him to follow through with the mission.

After the Ninevites repented and God spared them, Jonah was miserable. God sent Jonah a vine for shade, which cheered him up. God reversed the blessing by sending a worm to kill the vine, causing Jonah to wish for death. God brought to Jonah's attention how he is mourning the vine that gave him shade. God asked Jonah if he was willing to mourn a vine - *and how much more were the Ninevites worth?* Then, God asked Jonah if it was not worth it for God to give them a chance. Jonah did not answer, causing the reader to reflect on what it means for God to forgive their enemies. The forgiveness of enemies and using Jonah, who hated the Ninevites, again expresses the theme of God transforming wickedness into righteousness.

Activity 4

1. Choose one Old Testament prophet.
2. Summarize their story.
3. List the prophecies, warnings, and judgments they delivered.
4. Write about the lessons that can be learned from this account.
5. How does the prophet you chose link to the Old Testament themes of judgment, redemption, obedience to God, and using evil to bring about good?

The Covenantal System

A covenant is widely understood as a promise, but a more accurate way of looking at it is as a contract. God creates agreements with His people to bless them if they align to a certain standard and warns of the consequences of departing from those standards. In the Old Testament, there are four covenants before the fifth and final covenant of the New Testament under the sacrifice of Christ. The covenantal system includes the Noahic, Abrahamic, Mosaic, and Davidic covenants.

The Noahic covenant is the first in line. After flooding the world and ridding the planet of a wicked generation, God promised Noah that humanity would continue and that He would never destroy the Earth by water again. At the end of God's wrath and justice, mercy emerged in this Genesis account.

The next covenant comes through Abraham and is probably one of the most significant because it results in the birth of three major world religions: Judaism, Christianity, and Islam. God institutes the practice of circumcision, and for his faithfulness, God promises Abraham a nation and that the world would be blessed through his seed. God also promised that his people would receive land in which their nation could thrive.

The Mosaic covenant is the institution of the Law of Moses. As God delivered the Israelites out of Egyptian captivity, he gave them a law to govern their lives morally and ceremonially. The agreement was that if they were obedient, they would be blessed, and if they disobeyed, they would be cursed. The history of the Israelite people is framed through this lens of blessings and curses and a central theme of the Old Testament.

The last covenant before the coming of the Messiah, who saved humanity through grace and faith, is the Davidic promise, which is a continuation of the Mosaic Law. God promised to maintain the Israelites in the land if they obeyed Him but warned that they would go into exile if they departed from His ways and worshiped foreign gods. God also promised that a Messiah would come through the line of David, which would be the redemption of a fallen Israel.

Activity 5

Write down the details of each covenant and outline how it ties into the eventual coming of the Messiah in the New Testament.

_____

_____

_____

_____

_____

_____

_____

_____

_____

_____

_____

_____

_____

_____

_____

_____

_____

_____

Section 4: Wisdom Literature: Proverbs, Psalms, and Parables

The Bible is a multifaceted collection of books containing prophecies, law, history, mysteries, and practical wisdom. The wisdom literature deals less with grand revelations and more with the everyday lives of humans. As much as the details of the law can be understood, and the miracles of the text can be marveled at, they are sometimes not practically grounded. Therefore, the wisdom traditions of the scriptures provide a human perspective of work, family, and relationships as a way to navigate the complexities of the trials and triumphs resulting from life.

The books of Psalms, Proverbs, and Ecclesiastes, the parables of the Bible, give unique teachings in the wisdom tradition. These texts have common threads but differing perspectives, enabling the books to appeal to people in different stages of their lives with varying mindsets. These teachings are easy to understand because they are written to make them relatable to people. Although the texts were composed within a historical and cultural context, the messages they teach are relevant because some aspects of the human condition do not change.

Exploring the wisdom texts will give you an in-depth understanding of each book and how they emerged. You will learn how they applied to the people at the time, but, more importantly, you will reflectively engage with them so that they can be brought alive and grasped more deeply by interpreting them as practical and applicable guides. In this way, you can establish a link to the past by introspectively analyzing the text through the lens of your experience in the present. By relating the scriptures to your life, the wisdom books unfold into their fullness, allowing you to better embody the mentality of the authors and the audience they were speaking to.

Psalms

The Book of Psalms is a compilation of prayers, poems, and songs. Some works are anonymous, but different parts of the texts are attributed to various authors. Seventy-three Psalms are attributed to King David, a skilled poet and musician. One reason King David grew so close to Saul was his ability to soothingly play the harp. Other Psalms are attributed to Asaph, the sons of Korah, and the worship leaders of the temple, Heman and Ethan. Many texts in Psalms were sung as worship songs but not exclusively as hymns. The primary motivation for compiling the Psalms was to hold onto the spiritual traditions of Israel during the Babylonian exile. Therefore, the Book of Psalms emphasizes how Israelites should live in faith so that they can return to the Promised Land.

The Book of Psalms is a compilation of prayers, poems, and songs.[47]

Psalms can be logically divided into six sections, the first two Psalms being an introduction, encouraging meditation on the Torah's teachings, and reiterating the Messianic covenant established with King David.

Psalms 3 to 41 deal with covenantal faithfulness. Themes of blessings, curses, and mercy emerge as a constant thread in the Old Testament. In this section, you find one of the most popular texts in the Bible, Psalm 23:1, "The Lord is my shepherd, I shall not be in want." This Psalm emphasizes the reliance on God and total commitment to Him that Moses expressed in Deuteronomy 6:4-5 "Hear, O Israel: The Lord our God, the Lord is one. Love the Lord your God with all your heart and with all your soul and with all your strength."

The next grouping is Psalms 42-72, which expresses the hope for a coming Messiah after the exile the Israelites were experiencing. They depict how the Psalms' authors and compilers recognized that their captivity resulted from the wickedness that they embraced in the Promised Land – but that they held onto a brighter future in the new Messianic kingdom. This section concludes with Psalms 72: 1-2, "Endow the king with your justice, O God, the royal son with your righteousness. May he judge your people in righteousness, your afflicted ones with justice." This verse describes the institution of a Messianic kingdom. Notice the repetition of the word "*justice*," a literary device used by the poetry of Psalms. When Psalms' authors wanted to emphasize an idea, they often used repeating words.

The next section of Psalms spans from chapters 73 to 89, which outlines a hope for the coming of the Messiah amid the exile of the Israelites. Psalm 73:1 says, "Surely God is good to Israel, to those who are pure in heart." This may seem strange considering that Israel was under brutal Babylon rule, but it was a cry of hope that their liberation was near following the coming of a Messiah. Many of the Psalms compiled were written by David as a reminder of the promise God made to him to deliver a righteous king from his bloodline. The Israelites, under their oppression, needed to keep this hope of salvation coming through the bloodline of David alive. The Psalms compilation was created to allow the promises to resonate in the Israelites' collective memory. Psalms 90 to 106 emphasize God as the King of creation, instilling hope that the Israelites were in His hands and that He had the power to take them out of their oppression. Psalms 107-150 conclude the book with songs of praise.

The poetry of Psalms has a unique reflection style. Firstly, it draws back to some themes used in the earlier books, but it also interestingly mirrors itself. This mirroring is done by repeating words, like in Psalm 29:5, "The voice of the Lord breaks the cedars; the Lord breaks in pieces the cedars of Lebanon." The breaking of cedars is repeated for emphasis. A similar technique is employed to repeat ideas instead of words, like in Psalm 40:8, "I desire to do your will, my God; your law is within my heart." The idea of following God's will is repeated by highlighting the desire to do what the Lord wants. This is done by the author saying the law is in their heart and they want to do God's will, which is the same idea expressed in different words. This mirroring or repetition creates a unique poetic flow, allowing essential ideas to jump out at the reader using parallel pairings.

The ideas of redemption, hope, faith, the destruction of enemies, and the renewal of the glory of Israel through submitting to God are the key ideas of Psalms, expressed through beautiful poetic writing. Considering the historical context of this book's compilation of the Israelites in Babylonian exile, it makes sense that they would choose songs and poetry to communicate these ideas. The authors wanted the readers to memorize the texts to embody these principles. Hence, poetry was a better avenue than intense historical or narrative writing.

By poetically engaging with these ideas, the author gives the reader an entertaining and engaging way to grasp more profound teachings. Psalms is a brilliant book for a beginner to engage with scripture. Its practical nature and poetic language to emphasize key ideas make understanding easier than more complex prophetic doctrines requiring a baseline understanding of the law and the covenantal system. As part of the wisdom tradition, the Psalms dive more into everyday occurrences and classic wisdom that can be understood by people outside the culture, including believers and non-believers.

Activity 1

Write a poem exploring some ideas of Psalms relevant to your life. Draw on other writings of the Old Testament and use the poetic techniques employed in the book to emphasize your main message.

_____

_____

_____

_____

_____

_____

_____

_____

_____

_____

_____

_____

_____

_____

_____

_____

_____

_____

_____

_____

_____

_____

Proverbs

This intriguing book is one of the most defining scriptures for understanding Biblical wisdom. Most of the writings in Proverbs are attributed to Solomon. However, some are considered a collection of cultural knowledge predating the king. In addition to King Solomon, writings in Proverbs are attributed to Agur, son of Jakeh, and King Lemuel. The book is intertwined with the concept of wisdom, and Solomon's character is significant because, in 2 Chronicles 1:10, Solomon asks the Lord for wisdom so that he can lead his people well. Therefore, the king was intrinsically linked with this theme.

The Book of Proverbs was likely completed under the United Kingdoms of Israel during the 10th century BC. However, the compilation may have occurred later after the split, with the book being completed in the Southern Kingdom of Judah. Considering the cultural wisdom chain related to Solomon, some aspects of ancient Mesopotamia and Egypt also come out in the text. The personification of abstract ideas, like wisdom and folly indicative of the Proverbs writing, is a motif embedded in these ancient regions that may have influenced the writing style. If you consider the historical development of the religious idea of the Near East, then this amalgamation and cross-contamination is not surprising. The spiritual traditions of Israel were not birthed in a vacuum but came from common understandings and interwoven regional influences.

The Book of Proverbs specifically addresses young men, but timeless wisdom can be applied to people across time and cultural spectrums. Proverbs urges young men to decide wisely by basing their lives on submission to the will of God. Young men face two major temptations of folly according to Proverbs: the enticement to exploit people for wealth and falling into sexual immorality with women outside of wedlock.

Since ancient Israel practiced a collectivist culture, many of the wisdom teachings of Proverbs are framed through this communal understanding. The text teaches about having love for friends and the community and avoiding the exploitation of the most vulnerable in society, like widows, orphans, and the poor. There is a governmental element to the wisdom because Proverbs speaks about not using the courts or official structures to oppress people.

Proverbs is practical in its advice, outlining the perspective a young man should have if he wants to live a happy and fulfilling life. Proverbs highlights that a happy life is only found in the service of God. In addition to being happy, Proverbs emphasizes that living in submission to God is the only way to be useful. This extends through the Israelite understanding that conforming to the ways of God brings blessings, and departing from them brings curses.

Proverbs continues to clarify that God is not exclusively for Israel, but His wisdom extends throughout the world. This is why many of the teachings in Proverbs are also found in Mesopotamian and Egyptian schools of thought. The author purposely does this to emphasize that wise teachings are not merely confined to temples but should permeate every aspect of life. Proverbs is an early example of removing religious traditions from ceremonial practice, emphasizing that it is a way of life.

The community aspect of Proverbs is not limited to helping the vulnerable but comes forth in how it encourages young men to work hard and be humble. The wisdom tradition of Proverbs teaches that praise for your character and work should not come from yourself but should be invoked by those around you. It discourages laziness so that you can be a functional member of your community and contribute diligently.

Activity 2

Read the Book of Proverbs. Write a poem or short story that personifies wisdom and folly in your life as you reflect on the scripture's guidance.

The communal aspect of the wisdom of Proverbs is clear. How do you think official structures and social contracts exploit the most vulnerable in society today? How can it be avoided or remedied?

Ecclesiastes

Of all the wisdom writings, the Book of Ecclesiastes is uniquely naturalistic.[48]

Of all the wisdom writings, the Book of Ecclesiastes is uniquely naturalistic. The text is written in a way that acknowledges the complexities of the human condition and reveals profound truths about reality through this exploration. From the viewpoint of God, or human idealism, the world seems solid and should be fair. The wisdom books of Proverbs and Psalms emphasize the importance of making wise decisions for favorable outcomes. Ecclesiastes shatters that idealism with a dose of dark reality. No matter what you do, nothing is certain.

Regardless of what you seek in this earthly realm, it is all obsolete. Ecclesiastes explains that for the pleasure seekers, their moments of ecstasy pass, and misery will return at some point. Those who pursue wealth will exchange all their time for riches and may never get to spend it until they are too old to enjoy it. Then, they leave their inheritance to those who may have no interest in it. The Ecclesiastes author emphasizes that even the pursuit of knowledge is vain because the more you know, the more your sorrow increases since you now see the intricacies of the wickedness in the world.

This seems like a gloomy, nihilistic setup, but it is only to prepare the stage for the message of the entire Bible captured within this short book:

God is sovereign over all. Attempting to control the world and manipulate the outcomes of life is a fool's errand. The author acknowledges that it is preferred to follow the practical wisdom of Psalms and Proverbs but acknowledges that this does not guarantee anything. Like Job, who experienced difficulties despite being blameless, you must recognize that the Creator is sovereign.

Through all the highs and lows of being human, death knocks on everyone's door. The simple message to overcome the meaninglessness and unfairness of life is to keep God's commandments and fear Him. In this way, you take the burden of working out the complexities and paradoxes of life out of your hands and place that burden at the feet of the only one who could possibly understand, the Most High.

An artistic depiction of Death.[49]

Ecclesiastes is about understanding human limitations in a vast and confusing world. As much as people try to maintain the illusion of control, only God's grace brings them blessings, His mercy sustains them, and His judgment tears them down from high places. Centering a life on acknowledging that only God is in control is the Biblical concept of fearing God, repeated throughout the Old and New Testaments.

Often, people feel that their efforts get them to their position in life, but they forget that God's mercy is above the works of their own hands. Imagine a man who gets rich by carving intricate designs into furniture. He is highly respected, and his artwork is sought after by celebrities and politicians all over the world. He put in endless hours of practice and marketing to reach his current level. On the way home from a networking meeting, he gets into a tragic car accident and loses both his hands. All the hours spent perfecting his craft are now meaningless, and he must find a new way to earn an income. Regardless of his efforts, it is only God who gifted him the ability to prosper. As all his blessings came, God can take them away in an instant for reasons beyond human comprehension. The only constant that would make sense during and after the success is to honor God because He is in control. This is the core of Ecclesiastes' message.

Activity 3

List as many of your achievements in life as you can remember.

List as many of your failures as you can remember.

_____
_____
_____
_____
_____
_____
_____
_____
_____
_____
_____
_____
_____
_____

Reflect on how temporary these experiences are.

_____
_____
_____
_____
_____
_____
_____
_____
_____
_____
_____
_____
_____
_____
_____
_____
_____

Think about how much of what occurs in your life you can control and how much is beyond your control.

_____

_____

_____

_____

_____

_____

_____

_____

_____

_____

_____

_____

Through the lens of God's sovereignty, write about aspects of your life you should let go so that you can be guided by trust in a higher power.

_____

_____

_____

_____

_____

_____

_____

_____

_____

_____

_____

_____

_____

_____

_____

Parables

Teaching using parables is an ancient technique spanning cultures and times. Jesus is most well-known in the Bible for using parables to convey his message, allowing it to contextually resonate with His audience. However, the Messiah was drawing a long Israelite tradition of using metaphor to communicate powerful lessons.

The Biblical parable is structured in two parts. The first is the "*mashal*," when a short and engaging story is told. The second is the reveal, the "*nimshal*," the explanation allowing the audience to understand the parable. An example of this parable structure is when Jotham addressed the people of Shechem in Judges 9:7-15, referring to trees choosing a king among them. Jotham completes the parable in Judges 9:16-20 by comparing the imagery to the current political situation of the Shechem people.

Nathan uses this same parable structure when he rebukes King David for the wickedness he committed against Uriah by having an adulterous relationship with Bathsheba. Nathan started by telling the story of a rich man who stole the only lamb his neighbor had. David confidently stated how he believed that this terrible person deserved to be put to death. Nathan then revealed the nimshal by remarking that David was this wicked man, causing the king to repent.

Activity 4

Choose one of the consistent themes of the Old Testament. Use the structure of the mashal, followed by the nimshal, to construct a parable to communicate this scriptural theme. Use symbols and tropes in the parable that will make it relevant to a modern audience in contemporary times.

Section 5: The Prophetic Voices: Isaiah to Malachi

When people think of scripture, prophecy is probably the first thing that comes to mind. The Abrahamic traditions revere messages from prophets who act as God's mouthpiece on Earth. During the history of Israel, they went through specific social or political events. God communicated through prophets to address the people according to what occurred in the land. Prophets often referenced a future period where redemption or judgment would happen.

What Is Prophecy?

An accurate description of prophecy would be the message that God delivers to his people.[50]

People mistake prophecy for fortune-telling. Prophets tell of events that will occur in the future in the Bible, but this does not align with the scriptural understanding of prophecy. A prophet is like an ambassador for God, so a more accurate description of prophecy would be the message God delivers to his people. God works through a set order. What he communicates must flow through a hierarchy. Typically, God delivers a message to a prophet, which they will convey to the leadership or the masses, depending on the desires of the Most High.

Common Themes of Prophetic Messages

The minor and major prophets emphasize that God is sovereign over all. They come to warn people of a coming judgment due to their disobedience, injustice, and idol worship. Although many prophecies of the Old Testament contain terrifying warnings and descriptions of the wrath of God that could cause a person's heart to stop, they also come with possible redemption. God does not punish His people in vain. Every time Israel or other nations were judged, it was for them to repent of their wicked ways and return to righteousness. The narrative continued throughout the Bible, which is that God is making a way for His people to be redeemed, but it is balanced with justice because God's perfect mercy and fairness must be expressed.

Symbology of Prophecy

Common symbolic images emerge when Biblical prophecy is studied. Prophets often compare governments, nations, or key figures to beasts, emphasizing the carnal and destructive nature that the unjust take. Another repeated symbol that emerges is adultery or prostitution because grasping the covenantal system is easier than a marriage contract. A husband and wife commit to each other and make certain vows, and the rejection of extramarital affairs is one of the central tenets. Similarly, God commits to his people that He will bless and care for them, but they must follow his commandments and not worship idols or foreign gods.

Like a marriage destroyed by infidelity, God's relationship with His people is broken when they sway from their promises. However, God is like a forgiving husband who is merciful and always presents the opportunity for repentance so that His people can be redeemed. In apocalyptic writing, profound, esoteric symbolism is often used because prophets could not be found speaking out against empires and risking death. So, they had to keep their writings' meanings under wraps to allow only a select group to understand the text.

Major Prophets

The difference between major and minor prophets is not their importance but the length of the scrolls that refer to the details of their lives and prophecies. There are four major prophets and twelve minor prophets. The scriptures mention the existence of other prophets who spoke for the God of Israel and the gods of other nations, but they are not referred to by name. A prophet's position was taken on by many in the ancient world and was an important seat to fill. Since prophets were the mouthpieces of God, it is understandable why the Biblical text was concerned with separating false prophets from authentic ones.

Isaiah

Isaiah.[51]

Isaiah is one of the most significant prophets because of the messages he delivered about the coming Messiah. The nation of Judah had turned away from God when Isaiah was most active between 739 BC and 681 BC. They focused on ceremonial symbols and sacrifices but had completely abandoned the heart of the law. The people in Judah had become harsh and treated the kingdom's vulnerable with contempt. They had no love or kindness in their hearts, so their sacrifices were meaningless. Isaiah offered the most complete prophecies of a coming Messiah, who Christians believe was fulfilled by Jesus. His prophecies mentioned a virgin birth, and the child would be called Immanuel, which translates to "God with us." Isaiah highlighted Judah's lack of love, which was restored and fulfilled by the arrival of Christ.

Jeremiah.[52]

The books of Jeremiah and Lamentations are linked to this powerful prophet. Jeremiah functioned in the decades leading to the fall of Judah and their 70-year captivity in Babylon. By using the metaphor of adultery and prostitution, Jeremiah explained how Judah abandoned God by worshipping idols. Furthermore, Jeremiah prophesied that Judah's leaders were corrupt and oppressed the poor, widows, orphans, and immigrants.

Therefore, God used Babylon to judge the Israelites. Although Babylon was an evil empire, God used them to judge Israel, revealing the recurring Biblical theme of God transforming wickedness into righteousness. Jeremiah's warnings of judgment came to pass, which facilitated the Book of Lamentations, which recorded the events of the Babylonian exile and attributed the exile to their sin. Lamentations expressed Judah's grief and concluded with their repentance and hope for the future.

Ezekiel

Ezekiel.[58]

Under Nebuchadnezzar II's leadership, Babylon had begun taking over Judah during Ezekiel's prophecies. As a priest, Ezekiel was captured because of his high rank and kept as a servant in the city of Tel-Abib. As a vassal to the Empire of Babylon, Judah yearned for freedom, hoping to emerge victorious by collaborating with their Egyptian neighbors. On the Chebar riverbanks, Ezekiel received a vision of Israel's judgment and its neighbors, with Babylon as the tool God used. Ezekiel saw the presence of God leaving the temple in Jerusalem because of idolatry and corruption. However, he prophesied hope that God would redeem his people and restore the temple. The powerful imagery of dry bones lying in the desert depicts the current spiritual condition of God's people, and then the bones being restored with flesh depicts rebirth and restoration through God's redemption of His people. Ezekiel was a forerunner of apocalyptic traditions, making prophecies about the end times that were later repeated in the book of Revelations.

Daniel

Daniel."

Daniel, alongside other young men, was a captive of King Nebuchadnezzar. He prophesied when Judah was oppressed in Babylon for 70 years, as Jeremiah foretold. Daniel's faith remained strong throughout his life. As a teenager, Daniel was trained among the aristocracy of Babylon. His ability to interpret dreams won him favor from King Nebuchadnezzar and the rulers that followed. Jealousy among the elites got him thrown into a lion's den, but he emerged unscathed as a sign he was anointed. Daniel's prophecies used terrifying imagery of beasts to foretell about the kingdoms that would dominate the world and the events of the end times. Daniel's end-time prophecies relate to imageries in Revelations with the coming of the antichrist and the establishment of God's eternal kingdom that will rule over all other kingdoms.

Minor Prophets

The texts of the Minor Prophets are shorter than the Major Prophets but are not less important. The central message of prophecy is reinforced in these books. The theme of God blessing Israel when they keep His commandments and punishing them when they become unjust, unloving, and idolatrous is repeated in these short texts. It is unclear why more was revealed to some prophets and less to others, but the messages they delivered hold equal importance because they still come from God in the Biblical narrative. The symbolism used in the lives of the Minor Prophets communicates powerful messages. It clarifies the themes extended throughout the pages of the Old Testament, starting with the initial foundation of the Torah.

Hosea

This prophet began his work when Israel had already split into two kingdoms. Hosea operated in the Northern Kingdom. Hosea delivered prophecies of harsh condemnation by rebuking the elites who oppressed the poor and vulnerable and called out the idol worship of Israel. The Lord used Hosea's life as a symbol of how He interacted with Israel. Hosea's wife, Gomer, was a promiscuous woman. However, God did not call the prophet to rebuke her. God does the opposite, instructing Hosea to reconcile and have children expressing symbolic representation of God's relationship with His people. Even though they broke the covenant and metaphorically had adulterous relationships with other gods, the Lord still held faithful to his side of the covenant, ensuring that after judgment and turmoil, Israel would be redeemed.

Hosea.[55]

Joel

Joel.[56]

Joel was a prophet whose name meant "Yahweh is God." The prophet was active around 835 BC. When Joel came into the picture, the southern kingdom of Judah was in free fall economically, socially, and spiritually. When Joel was ministering, Judah experienced a devastating plague of locusts that ravaged the already struggling kingdom. Joel used this plague to highlight that worse was yet to come if Judah did not change its ways. He reinforced the idea that previous prophets mentioned how the Lord uses natural disasters and invading armies to judge nations that practice wickedness. Like many other prophets, Joel ended with a message of hope that all is not lost – *and calamity can be avoided.* He emphasized that if the people repent and return to the ways of the Lord, He will bless them, and they will not meet the tragic end that many other nations had decades prior.

Amos

Amos.[57]

The prophet Amos's ministry was short-lived, lasting less than a year in 760 BC. Israel had already been divided into two kingdoms, and Amos was from Judah. Amos was not recognized as a professional prophet in the religious structures but worked as a farmer. Since Amos did not belong to the religious structures, it allowed him to openly prophesize against them. He pointed out their hypocrisy because they observed rituals and ceremonies but exploited the poor to build their wealth. Judah was still small and was not yet threatened by bigger nations. Amos condemned Israel and their neighbors for their treatment of the poor, saying their injustice was a sign that they rejected God despite how they appeared outwardly holy.

Obadiah

INVADVERVNT ADVERS
VM· TE VIRI PACIS· TVÆ
QVI· COMEDVNT· TECVM
PONENT INSIDIAS SVPER
TE·
ABDIAS·P·

Obadiah.[58]

There is not much known about Obadiah's life. Due to the name being quite common, other mentions of the name Obadiah cannot accurately be linked to this prophet. Obadiah delivered his prophecy when both kingdoms had fallen, and Israel was in Babylonian exile. The Lord's judgment of Israel was clear, and the people mourned and repented. However, Obadiah preached hope by letting the people know their captivity was not the end. He prophesied that the day of the Lord was still to come, and the nations would be judged. He continued proclaiming that Israel would be restored, giving the broken people something to look forward to. Obadiah's prophecies highlighted that a merciful God would give his people another chance and open a pathway for redemption after judgment.

Jonah

Jonah was a rebellious prophet. The Book of Jonah is short, but it is one of the most popular stories in the Bible. Jonah tries to run from the prophecy he is meant to deliver to the Ninevites. However, his fleeing is futile because the Lord is in charge of the Earth. As he tried to escape, a storm ravaged the ship he was on. The pagans prayed to the God of Israel, and He revealed that Jonah was the reason for the turmoil. They threw

Jonah overboard upon the prophet's request, and they repented. A big fish swallowed Jonah, and in its stomach, Jonah prayed for salvation and promised to complete the mission. Through the story of Jonah's rebellion, God teaches that even pagan nations can be redeemed, and this lays the foundation for the message of loving your enemies, which was later preached by Christ.

Micah

Micah began his ministry in 721 BC. Israel had already split into the northern kingdom of Israel and Judah in the south. Micah predicted the fall of the northern kingdom. This prophet was a mysterious figure because not much is known about his life, and the Book of Micah does not present a narrative about his personal experiences. The prophet predicted the eventual fall of Judah, but he assumed it would be a lot earlier. Some central themes of Micah are the condemnation of false prophets and the rebuke of wayward leadership. Micah emphasizes that because Israel represents God's chosen people, it does not mean they are free from the consequences of their actions. Micah stated it is misleading to preach hope to the people when they are storing up God's wrath. Prophesying should be with God's timing, reaffirming the theme of the Lord's sovereignty.

Nahum

The Book of Jonah and the Book of Nahum work hand in hand. When Jonah warns the Ninevites that their city may be overturned, causing them to repent and be redeemed by God, Nahum prophesies their destruction. Nahum preached that the Lord is slow to anger, but like Judah and Israel were judged by the Lord, the Assyrians would face the same treatment. Ninevah's witchcraft and harlotry brought down God's wrath upon them. Nahum described in detail how the city would fall, and within 20 years of his prophecies, the events came to pass when the

Nahum.[59]

Babylonians destroyed the once mighty region. Nahum showed that God does not rule over Israel exclusively. He is the God of *the world*, reestablishing the Biblical theme of the Lord's sovereignty.

Habakkuk

Habakkuk.[60]

The height of Habakkuk's ministry was near the tail end of Judah before the kingdom fell. At this point, the Israelites in Judah became like the surrounding nations, partaking in idolatry and oppressing its most vulnerable citizens. Habakkuk was unique because he did not address Israel or its leadership. Instead, he conversed directly with God. Habakkuk struggled to understand whether God was truly good because of the injustice He allowed in Judah. God responded to Habakkuk, telling him that he would use Babylon to judge Israel, to which the prophet was appalled because the Babylonians were even worse. However, God reassured Habakkuk of His just nature by revealing that Babylon would also get judged for its actions. The main message that God gets through to Habakkuk is that he should trust the Lord entirely because He is just and sovereign.

Zephaniah

Zephaniah.[61]

Zephaniah traces his lineage back to Hezekiah, but other than this detail, little is known about this prophet. Zephaniah prophesied during the Josiah reign, who would be the 16th king of Judah around 640 BC to 609 BC. The prophet was probably active during the early part of King Josiah's reign because Assyria and Nineveh are mentioned in the book, but Babylon is omitted, so they may not yet have been a major threat to the southern kingdom. In the tradition of the prophets before him, Zephaniah noticed Judah straying from the ways of the Lord and warned of a coming judgment if they did not repent. Zephaniah also spoke of the day of the Lord, where there would be mass destruction, considered an end-times prophecy.

Haggai

Haggai's ministry began when a group of Israelites returned to Judah after the 70-year exile in Babylon. Cyrus of Persia defeated the

Babylonians and allowed some Judaens to return home under the Persian-appointed governor's leadership of Zerubbabel. Haggai had a vision of the restoration of the temple that was destroyed during the Babylonian conquest. Within five years, the temple was rebuilt and dedicated to the Most High. The reconstruction of the temple under the prophecies of Haggai demonstrates that after judgment comes redemption.

Zechariah

A central point of Zechariah's prophecies is the sovereignty of the Lord, a common thread throughout the Bible and foundational to an Israelite worldview. Zechariah opened the view of the Israelite God as sovereign over all nations and called everyone to submit to Him. This was revolutionary in the ancient world, where gods were viewed as being dedicated to specific geographical regions, and at some point, the Israelite God was understood in the same way. Many consider Zechariah's work as a foreshadowing of the coming Messiah that would open the final covenant beyond the Israelites and to the Gentiles.

Malachi

Malachi, like Haggai, functioned during the Israelite's return from Babylonian exile. This prophet spoke out against the behavior of the Israelite leadership, more specifically, the

Zechariah.[62]

Levitical priesthood. Many priests became decadent and indulgent, offering inferior sacrifices to the Lord, which could be traced back to Cain in Genesis, whom the Lord rebuked for not offering the first of his harvest. Furthermore, Malachi spoke against intermarrying with women from other nations who worshiped foreign gods, resulting in divorces being common. Malachi also called for the people to tithe more effectively because it was considered a doorway to blessings. Malachi highlighted Elijah as a forerunner for the Messiah and preached about the end times or the day of the Lord.

Relevance of Prophecy in the Modern World

When you study the prophecies delivered to Israel, its leaders, and those given to other nations, certain messages are repeated. According to scripture, due to the fall of humanity, it is likely that people will stray from the path God has set out for them. So, the same sins the Israelites embraced in the past - injustice and idol worship - will reemerge in contemporary times. Today, the world is becoming less religious, so it may not be clear what idols are in the contemporary age. However, the worship of material goods and the reverence of celebrities have replaced the Babylonian gods with whom the Israelites were enticed. Furthermore, there is mass injustice on Earth, with many of the rich exploiting the poor, keeping them in an oppressive cycle of poverty. Therefore, the prophetic message of the men of God is as relevant today as it was centuries ago.

Group Activity

Discuss in a group of four or five how the prophecies warning against idolatry and injustice and calling for repentance are relevant in the world today.

Journal Activity

Write down how the call for repentance, the warnings of the consequences of idol worship, and straying from the commandments of God are relevant in your life. Lamentations is a book of mourning and repentance. Include in your journal what you think you should turn away from and repent for.

Section 6: Dissecting the Gospels

The Gospels culminate the narratives established in the Torah, which continued in the historic, wisdom, and prophetic writings. God set up a covenantal system of laws, ceremonies, and celebrations. Central to this system was the practice of sacrifice. Many sacrifices exist in the Israelite tradition, but one of the most important was the Day of Atonement. This prestigious religious day has a whole chapter dedicated to it in the book of Leviticus. The Israelites became defiled throughout the year through their sins. So, on the Day of Atonement, a sacrifice was offered with the blood of an animal to cleanse the community.

The Gospels culminate the narratives established in the Torah, which continued in the historic, wisdom, and prophetic writings.[63]

Two goats were used in the ritual. The first goat was slaughtered and offered to God as a payment for the debt of the Israelite sin. A second goat that took on the sins of the community was released into the wilderness as a symbol of the transgressions of the year being carried away. The second animal, known as a scapegoat, is where the popular English literary phrase originates. For the Israelites to be forgiven, an eternal sacrifice was needed. Therefore, Christ came to fulfill that blueprint so that all people, at all times, could be washed clean of their sins.

Gospel is translated as good news or a good story. In Christian understanding, the crux of the good news is that Christ sacrificed Himself so that whoever believes in Him their sins could be redeemed. Most Christians believe that Christ is the Son of God and God in the flesh. To justify this position, they point to various New Testament references from Jesus's words and the apostles' teachings. They also point to Old Testament prophecies. Therefore, for believers, God establishes a new covenant, allowing all the nations to dwell in His presence through the sacrifice of His Son.

Historical Contexts of the Gospels

The church came before the written Gospel. Before the text was scribed, it was preached through oral traditions. These teachings were circulated among the early underground church, which was persecuted by the Roman authorities and some Israelite religious leaders. The Levitical priesthood once acted as a bridge connecting God to humankind through ceremonial practices and sacrifices. However, the new covenant of Christ, which allows you to go to God directly, challenged the authority that religious elites held. For the Romans, having people acknowledge a king above the Roman Emperor caused concern because it could have sparked a rebellion, which had occurred in previous uprisings led by messianic figures. So, in the Gospels during the life of Christ and in the books of Paul after His death, you see all these intersecting dynamics playing out.

Shortly after the ascension of Christ, it became necessary to record the Gospels to maintain the teachings since many in the Church were scattered and persecuted. Moreover, Israelites already had a strong tradition of recording scripture through texts, so the Gospels were a continuation in the same vein. However, like a game of silent whispers, the writings in the Gospel passed down through oral tradition caused some differences to appear in the text. Minor contradictions also occurred due to translation and scribal errors. Moreover, the scribes who wrote them down had their biases about which part of the story they wanted to emphasize. Lastly, there was the development of heretical Gospels like those of the Gnostics, a collective of ancient Christian cults. Many heretical groups promoted ideas fundamentally different from the orthodoxy of mainstream Christianity recognized today.

The Gospels of Matthew, Mark, Luke, and John are considered authoritative. Mark, Matthew, and Luke are called the synoptic Gospels. The word *synoptic* has etymological roots in two Greek words: "syn," which means together, and "optic," which means seen. So, it is best to study these works as a group due to their similarities and overlaps. The Gospel of John is a more spiritual book and does not fall under the banner of a synoptic Gospel. However, it is also valid. Arguably, because of its more spiritual and esoteric approach, the Gospel of John may have had some gnostic influences from early Christian groups that dealt more with the mysticism of the faith.

By the time the early church took shape, many conflicting Gospels were circulating. So, believers had to develop a way to determine which Gospels were authentic and which should be rejected as heresy. Early Christians used a variety of criteria to determine which Gospels were authoritative and which were not. The date when the Gospel was written was crucial because the closer it was to the life of Christ, the more likely it was accurate. Secondly, the early Christians rejected Gospels written under pseudonyms, which is why gnostic texts like the Gospel of Thomas and the Gospel of Peter were rejected. The synoptic Gospels and the Gospel of John were believed by early Christians to have been written by the authors claimed in the title. However, today, many Christians believe this was not the case and that these texts were also produced under pseudonyms. The last criterion was how widely the books were accepted. If they were used in many of the budding churches of the time, they were given more authority.

Christianity went through various phases. When the Gospels were written, the church was still a loose collective of scattered groups. The apostles and later the church fathers developed some doctrines of Christianity more clearly. Through this process, splits occurred, resulting in the many denominations today. The earliest formal churches were Orthodox and Catholic structures. The denominations that emerged from the Protestant Reformation and later disagreements are younger and were formed due to various disputes or beliefs. However, core teachings unite different groups. The most essential is confessing that Jesus is Lord, that He died for the sins of mankind, and that only through Him can salvation be obtained.

What Is the Central Message of the Gospel

The core message of the Gospel was established in the Old Testament through understanding the Lord's sovereignty. From Genesis to Malachi, the theme of God judging and redeeming nations is consistently repeated. It lays the foundation for a crescendo of ultimate redemption and judgment. The Book of Revelations was foreshadowed in the prophetic writings as the day of the Lord. This final judgment as restoration of God's Kingdom is outlined and will occur in the future. The ultimate redemptive process and covenant are established through Jesus Christ.

What drives God's mercy is love. The Old Testament symbolizes a marriage with the Israelites embracing adultery by worshipping other gods. Their injustice and exploitative treatment of the vulnerable highlight the lack of love, which is why the Lord called their hearts hardened. By accepting Christ, you are given a new heart. So, instead of working to earn the right to be closer to God, the Lord reforms you as you form a fellowship with Him. Therefore, it is not ritual and obeying the law that purifies you in the new covenant but a love for God that reforms your heart.

This is why the teachings of the Messiah are so focused on the doctrine of love. He criticizes the religious order of the day because they were mindlessly caught up in the details of the law but forgot its purpose. Moreover, much of Jesus's teachings are focused on the poor and vulnerable. The only time in the New Testament where you see Jesus violently losing His temper was in the temple when money changers and merchants were scamming people. You know they were not being honest in their dealings because Jesus accused them of being thieves.

Another core message of Jesus's teachings is mercy and forgiveness. In addition to dying for the forgiveness of sins, Jesus practiced the principles of grace and mercy before His death and resurrection. The popular story of the adulterous woman the village wanted to stone is the perfect indicator of mercy. Although the law commanded that she should be stoned, Jesus facilitated forgiveness by asking that the first person to throw a stone should be sinless. This is to emphasize that they, too, are not perfect and require mercy. Jesus came to remove the harshness from people's hearts and encouraged those who heard His message to find their humanity.

Jesus taught a radical love that is unmatched. Luke 23:34 highlights the remarkable love of Christ when the Messiah says, "Father, forgive them, for they do not know what they are doing." In the middle of being crucified and experiencing the most excruciating pain humanly possible, instead of cursing His persecutors, Jesus finds it in His heart to pray for their forgiveness. Many Christians focus on cleaving to Jesus for their salvation, which is essential, but it is often forgotten that while living, your actions should be driven by love, even to those who do you the most harm.

The fundamental message of Jesus's teachings in His earthly ministry was to start from the center point of loving God and extend that love to humanity. Next to the message of love, and intrinsically linked to it, was caring for the vulnerable. Jesus spent time among sinners and always preached blessings to the poor. When you think of the world today and how many Christians view the homeless, drug addicts, or prostitutes, it seems as if they have forgotten everything Christ stands for.

Who Is Jesus Christ?

The character of Christ changes according to whom you ask. Secular people study the Bible and conclude that Christ was a revolutionary Jewish preacher, but due to the miraculous claims of the Bible, they deny the supernatural aspects of the book. In Islamic tradition, Jesus is respected as a prophet, but claims that He is the Son of God or God in the flesh are rejected. Modern Rabbinic Judaism sees Jesus as one in a long line of charismatic, apocalyptic teachings that arose when Israelites lived under Roman rule. Through the Biblical lens, Jesus is the Son of God and God in the flesh who came to redeem the world.

Jesus Christ.[64]

The Christian conceptualization of Isaiah's words that a virgin would give birth and the child would be named Immanuel or "God with us" is that Jesus fulfilled this prophecy. Therefore, Jesus is the Messiah whom the nation of Israel had been waiting for. Many Israelites resisted this message – and still do today because they believe the Messiah would be a military or political leader, but they missed the spiritual aspect of sitting at the head of an eternal kingdom.

In essence, Jesus is the culmination of God's relationship with His people and all the nations of the Old Testament. The cycles of judgment and redemption all lead to the revealing of Christ as the Messiah. When God explains to Job that His ways are not easily understood, a part of the picture is revealed with the incarnation of the Messiah. The suffering, judgment, and subsequent redemption that God continually shows Israel is revealed in a cosmic form going back to Adam and the original sin. Before the kingdom is instituted on earth, God has made a way for His people to spiritually fellowship with Him through the blood of Christ.

Christ is the Word through which all was created. So, the restorative power of salvation comes through Him alone. No other sacrifice would have been worthy, so God had to come in the flesh for the completed work of the Old Testament to be manifested. Instead of focusing on a promised land, God expanded the conception of His kingdom to a spiritual realm so that wherever people find themselves, they can connect to His presence through Christ.

Parallel Reading of the Gospels for Common Themes and Stories to Emerge

The four Gospels of the New Testament were written within the first century after the death of Christ. The Gospel of John is the youngest and the most unique. There are many similarities between the synoptic Gospels, but the Gospel of John stands out. Unlike the other Gospels, where Jesus shies away from declaring His identity outright as God, He makes these declarations publicly in John. Furthermore, John opens with a more cosmological view of Jesus and does not spend much time on His early origins despite the virgin birth being miraculous. Of the four Gospels, John highlights Christ being on equal footing with the Father, emphasizing the eternal existence of the Son.

Mark is also unique among the synoptic Gospels insofar as it does not spend much time on the birth and early origins of Christ. However, there is much more overlap with Mark and the other synoptic Gospels than with John. Mark is the oldest Gospel in the Bible and the shortest, with some considering it a summary of the other Gospels. There is a view that Matthew and Luke were written using Mark as a source text, but this is not widely accepted.

Luke and Matthew have the most crossover. Some assume this may be because they share common authorship, but the most accepted view is that they were probably composed using the same source document called "Q," which has been lost to history. The synoptic Gospels include stories of Jesus casting out demons but are omitted in the Gospel of John. The divinity of Christ is emphasized in the Gospel of John, so it includes the most impressive miracles, like raising people from the dead and turning water into wine. The earthlier focus of the synoptic Gospels consists of the trial and arrest of Jesus, the final Supper, where Holy Communion was first instituted, and Christ praying for the bitter cup to be taken from Him. All four Gospels include Judas's betrayal of Christ.

Activity 1

Create a table or chart comparing and contrasting the four Gospels of Matthew, Mark, Luke, and John. Include their similarities and differences. Highlight which parts of the narrative each Gospel emphasized and summarize the core message carried through in all four texts.

GOSPEL	SIMILARITIES	DIFFERENCES
Matthew		
Mark		

Luke		
John		

Jesus in Contemporary Life

Jesus, in the Christian view, is the eternal sacrifice and the only gate through which the Father can be accessed. However, some contemporary progressive Christianity rejects the exclusivity of Christ as the way to access fellowship with God. Furthermore, some Universalist doctrines degree that Christ saves everyone, including those who reject Him. However, the faith's mainstream view accepts Christ as the only way to connect with the Father.

Christ preached that it is easier for a camel to pass through the eye of a needle than it is for a rich man to enter the kingdom of heaven (Matthew 19:24). Furthermore, when a rich man asked Him how he could be perfect in addition to following the law, Christ told him to sell his belongings and follow Him, which was too much of a burden for the man to handle (Mark 10:21-22). Considering the materialist outlook and the emphasis on acquiring wealth that permeates the global culture, including the church, some teachings of humility and the irrelevance of earthly treasure must be highlighted.

Social media and online entertainment have created an environment that encourages people to be more self-serving and self-centered. Christ emphasized that you should love others more than yourself. The Messiah did not place a magnifying glass on self-love but took on the most selfless act of sacrificing His life for the world. Even if a person does not accept the Biblical narrative as literal, the symbology of putting yourself before others is striking. The narcissism that is promoted by a self-obsessed culture is far from the example of Christ. If you consider that Christ is God in the flesh and He stepped down from His throne to dwell among humanity, thinking about how humble you are in this light can be transformative. The message of Jesus is eternal, so its application today is as new as when it was revealed two millennia ago.

The modern age is addicted to constant media, which encourages people to covetously compare lives. Some people emerge at the top and are put on a pedestal like the ancient kings who compared themselves to gods. If Jesus encourages people to love God above all and leave everything behind to follow Him, then these actions prove there is a clear misalignment with the scriptures. Jesus states that He will return not as a peacemaker but to judge the world, which begs the question of this modern idolatry and injustice that is storing up God's wrath in this age.

The Bible teaches that you should take the log out of your eye before looking to take the speck out of your brother's eye (Matthew 7: 3-5). When the Gospel is held up as a mirror, how well do you do? Intellectually studying scripture can be rewarding, but the true riches of the Bible are in its practical application. There is no better example than Christ in the narrative because He represents the fulfillment of all laws and prophecy. Therefore, when you measure yourself, Jesus should be the measuring stick. Although you will always fall short, which is why Christ's sacrifice was necessary, the life of a believer is built around striving toward the example of Jesus.

Activity 2

How can the teachings of Jesus to love your neighbor, love your enemies, and love God above all be applied in the modern era? What is meant by love according to the Biblical understanding? When answering this question, consider world events in the news and your personal life.

Section 7: The Book of Acts: The Growth of the Church

The period immediately after the resurrection and ascension of Christ was the liveliest in the church's development. The excitement and concern around this new, budding religion caused many controversies. Furthermore, like with any movement early on, what they believed and practiced was still being developed. The Biblical text Acts of the Apostles covers this vibrant and volatile period in the early church. Acts outline how the church was established under the leadership of Peter and the missionary activities of Paul.

A few main topics are covered in this engaging book, including the function of the Holy Spirit, the persecution of Christians, and the spread of the church to all nations. Where the Old Testament deals mainly with the story of Israel's relationship with God, the Gospels reveal how God is sovereign over all. Therefore, salvation was opened to the Gentile nations through the death and resurrection of Christ. When the views of gods were attached to nations and empires, this revolutionary idea that a God transcends geography, culture, and politics seemed radical. The Book of Acts contextualizes how this new and extreme idea spread and how people embraced this new revolutionary faith.

Authorship and Historical Context of the Book of Acts

The same individual who wrote the Gospel of Luke was responsible for the authorship of the Acts of the Apostles. Some argue it was Luke. Others say the Gospel writer used a pseudonym. Either way, textual analysis links both books to the same author. Acts were written after the Gospel of Luke between 75 AD and 95 AD. Many believe that other than Paul, Luke wrote most of the New Testament.

Although Luke was not an eyewitness to the ministry of Christ, he was a learned man who did extensive research interviewing people who witnessed the events. He traveled with Paul and likely met with many other apostles on his journey. Luke's professional background was as a physician, so he was among the highly educated class of his time. The systematic and detailed way he wrote is why he is regarded as one of the era's greatest historians.

Acts cover a large chunk of the early church's development, spanning over 30 years. The book outlines the 40 days after the resurrection until the ascension of Christ. It highlights Paul's conversion and how the Church's beliefs became solidified early on. The Acts of the Apostles highlight the function of the Holy Spirit, the third person of the Trinity, under most mainstream Christian doctrines. John 14:26 says, "But the Advocate, the Holy Spirit, whom the Father will send in my name, will teach you all things and will remind you of everything I have said to you." In Acts, you find the Holy Spirit moving in numerous ways so the church would be rightly guided in its infancy.

The geographical, political, and social setting of Acts occurs in the Roman Empire. The church spreads from the Near East in Israel into other Mediterranean parts of the Greco-Roman world in metropolitan cities like Corinth, Antioch, and Rome. The book further outlines how the religion spread into North Africa and the other travel routes that turned Christianity into a global faith. Although other missionaries are mentioned, Acts primarily focuses on Peter in the first half and Paul's work in the second half.

Acts highlights the triumphs and tensions within the early faith. It deals with issues like the baptism of Gentiles, whether they needed to keep the same purity law as Jews, and the struggles early Christians had against Jewish and Roman authority. The book ties into the Biblical theme of

God's sovereignty embodied in Peter's announcement that believers should follow the commands of God instead of the authority of men.

The Apostles and How They Grew the Catholic Church

It is easy to get swayed by denominational thinking when you approach the word Catholic. The first thing that pops into the mind when considering the word *Catholic* would be the Roman Catholic Church or the practice of Catholicism. However, this is a narrow view of the concept and the history of the church.

The establishment of the Catholic Church is the institution of Catholicism as the creation of a global church.[66]

The linguistic root of "Catholic" comes from the Greek "kata," which means "according to" and "holos," meaning "the whole." A simple way to understand it is that Catholic means "universal." Therefore, the establishment of the Catholic Church is not the institution of Roman Catholicism as it is denominationally understood today but as the creation of a global church. In the earliest days of the faith, there were loose Christian cult groups that studied whatever they could get their hands on and had many diverse beliefs. The establishment of the universal church under the operation of the Holy Spirit outlined in Acts is the story of how the church became unified.

When the church was in its budding stages, there was confusion. Christ had ascended, so the disciples who had followed him for the last few years were left almost without direction. However, before His departure, Jesus instructed them to go out into the world and be witnesses for Him. The beginning of church started in Jerusalem when many priests converted and abandoned temple service to become Disciples of Christ. As people saw their leadership now submitting under the apostles, they also joined, and the church grew exponentially. The church reached Cyprus and Southern Galatia from the starting point of Jerusalem. Next, the church spread to Greece and Ephesus. Eventually, the witnesses reached Caesarea and finally Rome.

According to the Biblical narrative, the Holy Spirit is responsible for the miraculous ability of small Christian cult groups to spread into a world religion. The start of the Holy Spirit's work to spread the faith in the Book of Acts began with Pentecost or the Feast of Weeks, a Jewish celebration 50 days after the Passover. Acts 2:1-3 describes the miraculous events that happened when the apostles were gathered at the celebration. The scripture describes a gush of wind, a thundering sound, and the strange occurrence of tongues of fire resting on them. A miracle occurred because all the men present could understand one another even though they spoke different languages.

This event can be linked to the Old Testament story of the Tower of Babel when the tongues of the nations were confused. The movement of the Holy Spirit now reunited the languages of the nations, not to do the desires of humankind but to promote the kingdom of God. The Holy Spirit resting upon the apostles and giving them the understanding of different languages and for people to hear what they spoke made them effective witnesses to go out into all the nations. There is debate about whether this verse should be interpreted literally or figuratively. Either way, from that point on, the decentralization of the Gospel was solidified, and the God of Israel became the God of the world.

Activity 1

Create a map of how the early church spread from a small corner of Jerusalem to Rome. Plot the key points according to Acts and explain what significant occurrences happened.

From Jerusalem to Rome: How the Faith Conquered the World

Before the ministry, death, resurrection, and ascension of Christ, the scriptures center belief in God around Israel. From the time of Moses, they look toward the promised land. Interestingly, although Moses played a pivotal role in delivering the law, he never entered the land. He led the Hebrews right onto the doorstep of Canaan, but Joshua was chosen to take them in after spending 40 years in the wilderness.

There was a key message the people missed, but Moses understood. It was never about the Promised Land but about dwelling in the presence of the Lord. This is why a journey that was meant to take a few weeks extended into decades. Even in the wilderness, the Israelites' needs were met because they were close to God. When they fell, God made a path of redemption.

In the story of Genesis, the progenitors of humanity were deceived by the serpent, which caused the fall. In the Torah, there is an account where Israel was attacked by serpents, and in order to live, they had to look toward a bronze serpent elevated on a staff. This bronze serpent was a precursor to Christ, who, in the new covenant, humanity had to look toward redemption. Like Christ was reflected in the bronze serpent, so too was the Holy Spirit reflected in the Tower of Babel's account of confusing the tongues of the nations to the Pentecost when the unity of the tongues of the nations was restored to spread the Gospel of Christ.

Therefore, through the Christian paradigm, the sole reason the church could spread from Jerusalem to Rome was because of God's presence or the Holy Spirit being with the apostles and early disciples. The division of nations God caused as a judgment was now restored through the united banner of the church. Under Christ, there was no more Jew or Gentile but one nation.

This declaration that Christianity puts humanity under one united national banner was controversial in the ancient world, especially considering the Roman Empire. Christianity spread fast, so eventually, the masses declared that the true king was Jesus. Roman society was conformist, so acknowledging a king above the Emperor threatened the Empire's stability. Hence, the early Christians faced persecution. Furthermore, the rabbinical Jewish system was under threat because a core teaching of Christianity is that you can access the Father directly.

Therefore, the scholarly and priestly classes were challenged, causing further friction.

These conflicts resulted in many arrests and martyrdom. Rather than hindering the growth of the church, early martyrs helped it to spread. Because people were willing to die for this belief, it created a mystique that enticed many to become followers. Therefore, the persecution of Christians had the opposite effect on Jewish and Roman authorities. This transformation of wickedness into righteous goals is an overarching theme repeated from the Old Testament, such as Jonah's disobedience, which brought pagans to call on the God of Israel.

Activity 2

Reflect on the significance of the apostles encountering the Holy Spirit at Pentecost to spread the Gospel to all the nations. Write about differences in how the early Israelites viewed salvation as national and how the new covenant of Christ opened redemption to all nations, including the Gentiles.

_____

_____

_____

_____

_____

_____

_____

_____

_____

_____

_____

_____

_____

_____

_____

_____

_____

_____

Mapping the Missionary Journeys of Paul

Paul's complete turnaround is one of the most drastic examples of an individual changing their path for God. As Saul, a Pharisee, Paul was on his way to Damascus to arrest and kill Christians. Before becoming Paul, Saul was born in Tarsus to strict religious parents who adhered to the Mosaic Law. Saul grew up to be a religious leader. He was committed to eradicating every Christian, believing he was acting on the will of God. Paul, blinded by religious conviction, would drag men and women out of their homes, violently throwing them into prison.

On the road to Damascus, Saul had a vision of Jesus asking why he was persecuting Him. The light of the Lord blinded Saul, who later went by his Roman name, Paul, so the Gentiles he was delivering the message to would receive him more openly. In his vulnerable state, unable to see, Paul followed Jesus' instructions and continued to Damascus to meet Ananias. At first, Ananias was afraid

Paul.[66]

because he knew of Paul's ruthless reputation. However, being faithful to God, he laid hands on Paul, who told him about his encounter with Christ. After Ananias prayed for Paul, he received the Holy Spirit and was baptized.

Once the primary condemner of Christians, Paul immediately went into the synagogues to proclaim Christ as king. Paul went from a ruthless killer and imprisoner of Christians to one of the most famous believers of all time. As his boldness grew, Paul preached the faith more widely. Paul preached in Damascus, Syria, and his home province of Cilicia. After Barnabas asked for his accompaniment, they went to Antioch.

Paul's main aim was to preach the faith to the Gentile nations, so he spent a lot of time among them. He was arrested in Macedonia after being falsely accused of inciting riots because he had cast demons out of a girl who followed him around chanting about how they were merchants of God, telling people how to get saved. The demon in this slave girl allowed her to have supernatural soothsaying abilities that were profitable for her owners. Therefore, after she lost the gift, their anger propelled them to seek vengeance on Paul, which landed him and Silas in prison. Paul's praise facilitated a miracle in prison when an earthquake swung all the doors open, but none of the prisoners escaped.

The second time Paul was arrested was in Jerusalem. Paul faithfully preached the Gospel wherever he went. However, because he taught the Gospel to Gentiles and told them that they did not have to get circumcised or keep Jewish purification laws, the religious authorities again falsely accused him of telling Jews to abandon their traditions. To prove the religious leaders wrong, he went along with Israelite men to complete purification rituals but was arrested for bringing Gentiles into the temple and taking Jews away from their customs. These accusations were false.

While standing trial in Jerusalem, the religious leaders became excessively violent, which prompted Roman authorities to take Paul to Caesarea. Eventually, Paul went under house arrest in Rome where he wrote the epistles to the various churches. The end of Paul's ministry came when he was martyred in Rome, but his work had by then spread the faith far and wide.

Activity 3

Often, the Old Testament speaks about hardened hearts. Through Christ, the Bible provides a way to receive a heart of flesh to replace a heart of stone. The transformation of Saul to Paul perfectly embodies this exchange. Comment on the differences in Paul's character and mindset after he encountered Christ.

_____

_____

_____

_____

_____

_____

_____

Activity 4

Create a map of Paul's missionary journey, including when he was in prison. Highlight the significant occurrences that helped spread the Christian faith.

_____

_____

_____

_____

_____

_____

_____

_____

_____

_____

_____

_____

_____

_____

_____

_____

_____

_____

_____

The Ancient Church and The Modern Church

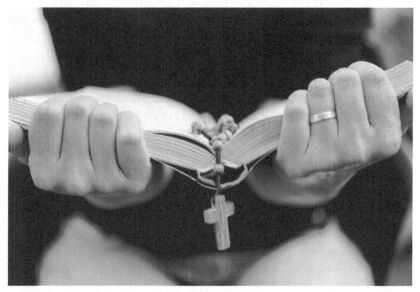

Christianity is the most widely practiced religion in the world.[67]

Christianity is the most widely practiced religion in the world, although, in some parts of the world, Christians face heavy persecution. However, the faith has become mainstream in many nations. Being a Christian in the ancient world was a death sentence, but people could not hide underground because the scriptures commanded the Gospel to be shared. This meant that many of the earliest followers of what was then called "the Way" were signing their own death warrants. This martyrdom was one reason Christianity spread so fast because once the masses saw that people believed in this idea so strongly that they were willing to die for it, many converts were won over.

Like the modern church, there were disagreements during the infancy of Christianity. The faith began in Jerusalem and was first mainly comprised of Jewish people. However, Paul and Barnabas won over an increasing number of Gentile believers. Arguments circulated about whether it should be required to get circumcised. They concluded that Gentiles did not have to get circumcised or align with Jewish purification laws to become Christian.

The principle that allowed Gentiles to keep some of their customs and Jewish converts to keep practicing their own traditions showed that the Christian faith was meant to be open for all nations to be united under Christ. Evidence of this multicultural foundation is alive today when you see nationalities practicing Christianity unique to their cultural identity. For example, the Ethiopian Orthodox Church has an African way of worshiping in its iconography and the drum rhythms it uses during mass, and the glitz and glamor of many charismatic churches have a modern American feel.

The early church pooled many of its resources together and functioned like a community. It was quite different from modern churches that put money together for activities and to maintain church buildings but did not live communally as early believers did. The early church was a community, whereas churches today form part of a broader community. There was more unity in the early church because the idea of a catholic or universal church was embraced more profoundly. Later developments brought along many schisms and conflicts, leading to the present-day denominations.

Activity 5

Now that you have studied Acts and the spread of the early church, are there any significant differences between the church then and now? If so, what are they?

_____

_____

_____

_____

_____

_____

_____

_____

_____

_____

_____

_____

_____

_____

_____

How do you think the modern church can be reformed to align more with the original church after the Holy Spirit at Pentecost?

_____

_____

_____

_____

_____

_____

_____

_____

_____

_____

_____

_____

_____

What are the similarities between the ancient church and the contemporary church? What are the positives and negatives of those similarities when weighed under the criterion of producing committed believers?

_____

_____

_____

_____

_____

_____

_____

_____

_____

_____

_____

_____

How can the positives be enhanced and the negatives be diminished?

_____

_____

_____

_____

_____

_____

_____

_____

_____

_____

_____

_____

Section 8: Wisdom from the Epistles

Epistle is another name for a letter the apostles wrote to the church for correction, clarification, or encouragement. In the early days of the church, the movement was growing, and so much guidance was needed from the apostles to whom Jesus had entrusted to build His congregation. The growing pains of the church and the convert's multicultural nature created confusion and arguments. Therefore, the apostles had a job to clearly define the message of the Gospel and how to practice the faith correctly. These letters address the difficulties of the early faith, which the modern church experiences today. Therefore, studying these letters can provide deep insight into the practical intricacies of Christianity and reveal how the church was established historically.

The Pauline Epistles

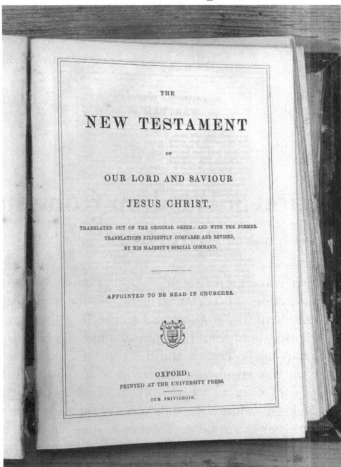

The New Testament includes the Pauline epistles.[68]

As the name suggests, the Pauline epistles are the letters included in the New Testament written by Paul. Some of these books were not authored by the apostle but used him as a pseudonym to give the books more authority. This may seem odd today, but it was a common practice in the Middle East and Mediterranean at the time. The epistles of Paul are divided into four groups: the authentic Pauline, Deutero-Pauline, Pastoral Epistles, and one anonymous sermon some attribute to the apostle. What makes the Pauline epistles unique is that most were addressed to specific regions and people, as opposed to the general or catholic church. These were the letters Paul wrote on his global missions and when he was under house arrest in Rome.

Authentic Pauline Epistles

The first of the authentic Pauline epistles is Romans. The main message the apostle focuses on in this letter to the Roman church is salvation. Paul describes that you are saved through faith in Jesus Christ, meaning you could not earn salvation through good deeds. Paul explains that once you believe in Christ, you will be reformed and exhibit gifts to build up the Christian community. The Roman church was ethnically diverse because it was in the center of the Empire. So, this letter was likely heard by Gentile and Jewish converts in Rome. Considering the diversity within the Roman church, Paul emphasized a unified identity to get the church in the great metropolitan to work together through the unifying force of Christ despite their differences.

Paul heard that the church in Corinth was going down a wayward road, so he composed the first epistle of Corinthians to offer guidance and correction. The apostle was on a missionary trip in Ephesus when he received a letter from the church in Corinth that concerned him. A member named Chloe wrote to Paul, informing him about quarreling in the church and providing other details about what was happening. The letter was written around 55 AD and addressed to the church in the city Paul had founded while there. The congregants had become prideful and justified sexual immorality. Paul provides the most exhaustive Biblical definition of love in this letter in 1 Corinthians 13:4-7. He explains to the church how they acted worldly with their infighting and behavior. Paul describes how the body is a temple and how the church's conduct should reflect their born-again nature. The main message of this letter is that everything the church does should be for the glory of God.

The second book of Corinthians is a continuation of the first epistle Paul wrote to this church. After hearing how the church of Corinth had corroded, the apostle made a journey to the city. After visiting the church, Paul went back to Ephesus and wrote to them again, expressing his sorrow. However, this letter has been lost to the passage of time; 2 Corinthians is a letter Paul wrote while in Macedonia after Titus sent him a report of good news of improvements in the church. This letter was written around 56 AD. In this second epistle, Paul reinforces the idea of unity after many in the Corinthian church repented of their wicked ways. However, some congregants had found Paul's humble nature concerning, so they doubted his authority. Therefore, Paul reinforces his role by emphasizing that he is just as important as the other apostles and gives some details about his life. The apostle highlights that forgiveness and reconciliation are the cornerstones of maintaining the church.

In 51 AD, Paul founded a church in Galatia, which is part of Turkey today. Paul writes to the church in Galatia because numerous false teachers had sprung up claiming that to be Christian, believers must observe the purity laws given to Israel in the Old Testament. Paul's message to this church is that they should focus on the saving grace of Christ through faith in Him instead of falling victim to legalistic false teachers. The mixture of Jews and Gentiles in the church created a theological issue concerning the importance of the Mosaic Law. One group insisted that to be saved, Gentile converts had to be circumcised. Paul rejected these claims in this letter by highlighting that faith in Christ is the only way to redemption.

Paul was incarcerated in a Roman cell while writing Philippians. Conditions today in modern jails are like a five-star hotel compared to ancient prisons. So, you can imagine how much the apostles suffered. Amid this hardship, Paul wrote to the church in Philippians to emphasize joy, which seems counterintuitive. Paul highlighted that there is an abundance of joy in being a disciple of Christ, and regardless of what people go through, the service of the Lord is uplifting. This message is especially profound and inspiring, considering Paul's dire circumstances.

The first book of Thessalonians is the earliest of Paul's letters, dating back to 51 AD. Paul wrote to Thessalonica a few months after establishing the church in the region. When the apostle wrote to the Thessalonian church, he was on a mission in Corinth. Of all of Paul's letters, this one speaks clearly about the end-times events. He highlights the return of Christ and how believers will be united with Him. Paul provides words of encouragement because the Thessalonians remained faithful despite persecution. Paul might have mentioned the return of Christ in this letter to give the church struggling under oppression something to look forward to.

Paul addresses this letter to Philemon, a leader in the Colossians church, instead of addressing the church in general. From the letter, you can tell that Paul and Philemon had a close friendship. Philemon was an early Christian slave owner who hosted a church in his home. One of the more controversial aspects of the Bible, often emphasized by critics, is that there is no outright condemnation of slavery in the New or Old Testaments. However, the practice was common at the time, so it was not frowned upon like it is today. Paul sent Onesimus, a runaway slave, back to Philemon, asking his friend to receive him with grace because he was now a believer. The letter emphasizes that even in a master-slave relationship, love must be shown among believers.

Deutero-Pauline Epistles

The Deutero-Pauline epistles are in line with the ancient tradition of the early church, where pseudonyms were used to give texts higher authority. Although Paul did not author the Deutero-Pauline letters, and some would call them forgeries, they form part of the Biblical canon. The Deutero-Pauline epistles shared common themes with Paul's authentic letters and were likely inspired by them. These letters include Ephesians, Colossians, and 2 Thessalonians. Furthermore, the pastoral epistles of 1 Timothy, 2 Timothy, and Titus are part of this group because the scholarly consensus is that Paul never wrote these books either (Ehrman, 2009). Although these letters were likely not written by the apostle, they may have been composed by his followers, so their teachings are considered valuable, so they are included in the Biblical canon.

Although the modern scholarly consensus is that the Deutero-Pauline letters were not written by Paul, they are constructed in a way that seems like his apostles wrote them. Many believe these letters were written by one of Paul's followers after his death. The Epistle of Ephesians was likely written sometime in the 60s AD. The writing of Ephesians under the pseudonym of Paul again calls for unity in the church, saying believers should be committed to God first and should also be committed to one another. The letter encourages believers to remain steadfast in their faith despite their struggles.

Thessalonians 2 is another letter that may not have been written by Paul but contains the same teachings. This letter speaks to the church's fear that the return of Christ had already occurred. The writer assures the church that Christ has not yet returned and provides signs to look out for to know if it is the second coming. The author writes about a great falling away from the faith that will occur and introduces the concept of the antichrist or, as the letter refers to, "man of sin" and "The son of perdition." People argue whether this refers to a system or an individual. Thessalonians 2 is heavily concerned with the signs of the end times.

Colossians is the last of the Deutero-Pauline epistles that do not fall into the pastoral category. It focuses on the sufficiency of Jesus for redemption and salvation. Some believe Paul wrote this letter from prison, but the scholarly consensus asserts it was likely one of Paul's followers who composed it after his death. The church in Colossae was experiencing a plague of false teachings, including Jewish legalism and mysticism. Therefore, the letter emphasizes that the death, resurrection, and ascension of Christ are central to the faith, and anything else added to that is unnecessary. The author encourages the Colossians to trust in their faith in Christ instead of trying to earn salvation through other means.

Pastoral Epistles

The pastoral epistles address leaders in the early church. They are predominantly concerned with structures, organization, and sound doctrine. These letters instruct how a church should be run, its operations, and what is expected from the members and leadership. The pastoral epistles include the first and second Timothy and Titus. These books form part of the Deutero-Pauline tradition because they use the apostle as a pseudonym. However, many modern scholars have determined that the books were written by followers of Paul and not by him directly. If you consider how communally early church members lived, it is almost as if pastoral epistles are governmental documents rather than constitutions.

According to the opening verses of 1 Timothy, it was written by Paul to Timothy while he was in Macedonia. However, there is evidence in the text that it was produced later. For instance, the linguistic structure of the letter aligns more with second-century writing than the time it claims to be from, so it was likely written pseudonymously. The work has some gnostic elements, putting a lot of emphasis on the ascetic parts of the faith. The letter mentions different positions in the church, including bishop, deacon, and elder. It speaks of widows and how they should be given financial support by the congregants, again emphasizing a collectivist attitude among worshippers. A more controversial part of the letter is the assertion that women should remain silent in church, which has caused modern debate about whether women should take up office.

The second book of Timothy reiterates ideas put forward in the first epistle of Timothy. Again, the leader is encouraged to stand on the true teachings of Christ, shunning anything immoral. The false teachers who reject Christ are compared to individuals who crafted the golden calf in Moses's time. The letter highlights how these idol worshippers died and states that those who reject Christ will meet a similar fate. Although the letter is written under a pseudonym, it is presented as the last words of

Paul, who was aware he would soon die under Roman imprisonment. Instead of expressing concern for his situation, he focused on the church, reinforcing the selfless and collectivist attitude believers should embrace.

The letter of Titus is written as if it were the words of Paul, but modern scholars reject the idea that these were the words of the apostle, asserting that it is a work produced after his death. However, the same ideas contained in the undisputed letters are present. In this letter, the author addresses Titus, one of Paul's companions in Crete. The writer emphasizes that although Christians live in a Godless culture, they can resist these temptations and hardships by being reformed by their belief in Christ. Titus was tasked with removing false teachers and replacing them with Godly people to direct the church in the right direction.

Anonymous Sermon

Although some attribute the letter of Hebrews to Paul, the book does not explicitly list the author. The scholarly consensus is that it belongs not to Paul but rather to another unknown author, which is why it is considered an anonymous sermon. One theory is that this was a sermon Paul preached, which was later recorded in this book. The main message of this letter was for Jewish followers of Christ to hold onto the new covenant under the Messiah instead of returning to the Old Testament ways.

Activity 1

Break into groups of three or four. Assign an epistle to each group. Discuss the main message of your chosen epistle and present the information in a creative role-playing scenario by putting yourself in the position of the church community receiving the letter.

Catholic or General Epistles

Most letters in the New Testament were written by Paul or at least pseudonymously claimed to have originated from the apostle. The general epistles are letters written by other church leaders at the time. The general or catholic epistles were usually not addressed to a specific person or group but for distribution among the wider church body. The letters establish orthodoxy of how a church should be run and the principles or structures the body of Christ should embrace. They mirror many of the same messages in the Pauline epistles, showing that a common understanding of the faith emerged early on.

Epistle of James

The letter of James was written shortly before the 49 AD council of church leaders in Jerusalem, which determined the Gospel should be spread to Gentile nations. This letter resembles the wisdom literature of the Old Testament, which focuses on the more practical aspects of Christian living. This connection to the Old Testament makes sense because a large section of James's audience would have been Jewish. The main message of the letter was that faith should permeate every part of a believer's life.

First and Second Epistles of Peter

Peter was one of the most important apostles because Christ personally commissioned him to be the rock on which the Church was built. Peter is considered the first Pope in the Roman Catholic tradition. The epistles of Peter were likely written after the death of Paul. The letters of Peter promoted the idea that Christians scattered throughout the world are the chosen people of God, reinforcing the concept that Christianity is not a nationalist faith like many predating religions. Peter encouraged Christians to remain strong in their struggles, live virtuous lives, and avoid false teachers.

First, Second, and Third Epistles of John

The Epistles of John were written between 85 AD and 100 AD, so they led the church into the second century. Since many Christian cults with contradicting beliefs were forming in this era, John was concerned with establishing orthodoxy among the catholic or general church. John condemned teachers who denied the bodily resurrection of Christ and rejected those like Diotrephes, who denied apostolic authority. John established a Godly order that the church should follow for unity of beliefs and structure.

Epistle of Jude

Jude, who was a church leader in Jerusalem, was likely the half-brother of the Messiah. The letter is not focused on a specific region but addresses all believers. This letter was written between 65 AD and 80 AD. The primary purpose of Jude was to warn Christians about false teachers penetrating the church to promote evil doctrines. Like the other epistles, Jude encourages believers to persevere while refraining from false teachers exhibiting ungodly behaviors, like chasing status, constantly complaining, and following their desires instead of the instructions of God.

Non-Canonical and Lost Epistles

You can tell that some letters written by apostles to the church have been lost. Paul references previous letters in Corinthians, but these epistles have not been found and are not part of the Biblical canon. Some letters dated to around the same time as many of the works in the Bible, but they did not make it into the canon for various reasons. The practice of writing letters of encouragement and correction to the church did not end with the early apostles. The church fathers of the first and second centuries wrote many letters to various churches, which helped shape how Christianity is viewed today and assisted in defining some of the foundational doctrines of the faith.

Activity 2

Using the style and tone of the New Testament epistles, write a letter to a modern church community addressing some of the themes explored in these scriptures.

Activity 3

Create a chart to compare and contrast each apostle's teachings on faith, leadership, and forgiveness. Note the similarities and differences so that you can unveil the different approaches of each apostle.

APOSTLE	SIMILARITIES	DIFFERENCES

Section 9: Understanding the Book of Revelation

The Book of Revelation is the most symbolic and esoteric scripture in the Bible. Although Old Testament prophecies from Isaiah and Ezekiel used the same coded language, the mystery of Revelation has captured the interest and imagination of many worldwide. Humans in various cultures throughout the ages have always been obsessed with the world ending. Many myths and stories have been composed about how the destruction of creation will ultimately come about. The Book of Revelation aligns with this ancient intrigue of humanity meeting its end. Considering the persecution the early church faced and the oppression of the Israelites under Roman rule, it is easy to see why many at this time would want to know about the signs of the end. Revelation paints a descriptive and symbolic picture of what will happen in the last days and what believers can expect and should prepare for.

The Book of Revelation aligns with this ancient intrigue of humanity meeting its end.[69]

History and Literary Structure of Revelation

The Book of Revelation was written after Jerusalem was destroyed by the Romans in 70 AD. Therefore, the Jewish community and Christianity, essentially an apocalyptic sect of Judaism, became a real concern. Revelation was written between 90 AD and 100 AD. Most scholars date it to about 96 AD. The book was written by John the Elder, known as *John of Patmos,* because it was where he got the vision. There is no indication in the scripture that this John is the same person as the apostle John. They were likely two different people because of the time frame. Furthermore, John was a common name.

It is difficult to understand the meaning of Revelation because modern people are so far removed from the cultural context in which it was written. John was writing to a specific audience of believers who were likely able to understand and decode the symbols of the book far better than people today. Many read Revelation by piecing together prophecies of the past to create a bigger picture. However, this exercise is highly speculative. It is best to study the text as a self-contained unit to get the clearest picture of its meanings.

Revelation is written to seven churches in the Roman-controlled region of Asia Minor, known as Turkey today. John received visions on the island of Patmos, off the coast of Turkey. The writer was likely exiled to the island for his work in spreading the message of the Gospel, which the Roman Empire would have seen as disruptive. The text was written in Greek, which was widely spoken among the Christian community.

The church was experiencing a tumultuous period, which John highlighted in the book's opening chapters. Christians in Smyrna and Philadelphia were socially shunned and widely denounced, placing them in danger of death or imprisonment. The church communities in Ephesus, Thyatira, and Pergamum had trouble integrating and assimilating into the pagan cultures surrounding them. For example, they had to question the morality of eating food sacrificed to idols. The last churches John addressed were in Sardis and Laodicea. These congregations were prosperous and thriving. However, the author referred to them as spiritually dead. Their faith had diminished, so the author attempted to revitalize their zeal for the Lord.

Christians in the Roman Empire clashed with the imperial forces because they could not conform to the Empire's requirements. People were allowed to practice religions of their choice in the Roman world.

However, since Rome was a conformist culture, they still had to participate in the Empire's broader practices. The Emperor was worshipped as a god on Earth, and many temples were built to be devoted to him. Although the public was allowed to worship gods of their choosing, they had to partake in the Empire's religious rituals to create a unified identity. Christians were not allowed to because they saw Christ as the true king and followed the Old Testament prescription to worship no other gods other than YHWH, the same reason the Jewish people clashed with the Empire. Jews and Christians refused to bow to the Emperor as God. Therefore, much conflict and persecution occurred due to this tenet of the religion.

For many in the Christian and Jewish world, this felt like the end, as if God's judgment was falling onto them. Therefore, although the symbolism of Revelation can seem scary and violent, a message of hope is embedded in the book, aligning with the scriptural tradition of encouraging people during hard times. It echoed the tradition started in the Old Testament to maintain faith by trusting in God's sovereignty.

Revelation was written when many Christians were killed for their beliefs and practices. Rumors circulated, and propaganda spread that Christians were wicked rebels looking to overthrow the Empire. Therefore, John emphasizes martyrdom in the text not to push believers to die for their faith but to encourage them to persevere regardless of the political persecution.

Revelation ties spirituality, prophecy, religion, and politics together tangibly by using symbolic language. It is easier to grasp a narrative than to follow a list of bland instructions. Although the story structure of Revelation is not linear, it is captivating enough to hold attention. The powerful symbols used to describe the world and the future of Christianity are why Revelation is one of the most studied texts in the Biblical canon. The scripture was composed to get the people of that time to keep pushing forward and look to the future, but the message resonates with so many today who expect many of the prophecies to be fulfilled and see the writings as a reflection of the modern world.

Activity 1

Construct a timeline of the prophetic visions in Revelation. Research and speculate on what these end-times visions could mean and whether these signs are present today.

Symbology and Interpretations

The Book of Revelation's symbols hold the attention of so many. The book does an amazing job of creating an encoded and symbolic world, from terrifying spiritual and political leaders to monsters and feminine personifications. Some speculate that the encoded language was meant to get Christians to understand it while hiding its true meaning from Roman forces that would aim to stop its spread. Controversies exist around how Revelation should be interpreted due to its deep, esoteric writing. Some assume the book can be understood as a description of the then-Roman world. In this understanding of the text, the prophecies refer to events John believed would occur in his lifetime. Others interpret Revelation as occurrences that will happen far into the future.

Revelation is not written in a logically structured way. The text is written almost dream-like, illogically jumping from one vision to the next in a non-linear fashion. The surreal imagery is captivating, but following along in a story format is difficult. Therefore, piecing together Revelation explanations and placing them onto the historical context's blueprint is necessary. In this way, the symbology of the text can be decoded.

An interesting exploration of Revelation's meaning is its use of numbers to communicate various messages. For example, the text mentions seven churches. Biblically, the number seven represents holiness and completion. So, although the writing might have been addressed to seven churches, it could symbolically indicate that John intended it to be written for the entire body of Christ. Seven is repeated as the seven spirits that burned before God's throne and the seven eyes of the Lamb representing Christ. Therefore, Revelation positions itself as a complete representation of prophecy with multiple uses of seven in the text.

Another repeated number is 12, which represents the followers of God. The 12 disciples and the 12 tribes of Israel all paint the picture of being chosen by the Lord. The number is repeated in the text, with 144000 representing God's people that will enter the 12 gates of New Jerusalem. When you divide 144000 by 12, it is equal to 12000, which is a repetition of the number that emphasizes the link to being under God's nation. The number 666 in Revelation is described as the number of the beast that will mislead the world. Some believe this is not the number of prophesied antichrists in the future, but it represents Nero, the Emperor at the time.

It is difficult to map out a timeline of Revelation, so many theologians and scholars develop conflicting narratives. The fluidity of the time in the dreamy, almost nightmarish visions of John creates a wispy feel, making it challenging to grasp a particular thread to follow. The text jumps around confusingly, indicating that John was writing down what he saw instead of creating a solid story structure to follow.

Revelation uses animals and monsters as symbols. Christ is compared to a lamb because of His sacrifice, and the whiteness of the wool represents purity. Satan and the wicked system are depicted as devouring beasts that come to terrorize and destroy. The climax of this imagery is Christ switching from the vulnerable lamb sacrifice to someone who will destroy the wicked powers of the world. It describes a sharp sword coming out of the Messiah's mouth to destroy the nations. This likely indicates that political decrees will be made to free Christians before establishing the Kingdom of God on Earth.

The controversial reference to the "synagogue of Satan" in Revelation has been used throughout history to persecute Jewish people by fueling anti-Semitic tropes. However, the author did not intend to demonize the Jewish community because many Christians were Jewish converts. It was probably done to highlight Jewish leadership's collaboration with Roman authorities because the budding Christian movement presented a challenge to their power and put some under their rule in danger by attracting unnecessary Roman attention.

Ultimately, Revelation, with all its deep symbology, is a complex comparison between the powers of the world and how believers should conduct themselves. The persecution experienced by Christians at the time could easily have discouraged them, so Revelation provides hope for a brighter future and justice for those who killed and oppressed them. The comparison is best embodied in the contrast of the whore of Babylon representing the evil powers and the daughters of Jerusalem or the bride of Christ representing the believers. The contrast between a faithful bride and a blasphemous, adulterous whore vividly depicts how far Christian conduct ideally is from the wickedness of the nations that oppress them.

Activity 2

Interpret the following symbols in Revelation:

- Whore of Babylon.
- The Beast from the Sea.
- The Beast of the Earth.
- Image of the beast.
- 666.
- Bride of Christ.
- Seven Seals.
- Seven Trumpets.

Early Christian Understanding of the Book

Considering what occurred then, it is unsurprising that a devotee of the scriptures would write an apocalyptic text. Shortly before Revelation was written, Mount Vesuvius had erupted, Jerusalem had fallen, and the Roman authorities persecuted Christians. The end of the world seemed right next door for ancient believers. Apocalyptic literature is not foreign to the Biblical consciousness because Israel had established a long tradition of prophetic writings in the Old Testament and the epistles. Therefore, the writings of John would not have been seen as odd but offered a lifeline to believers in uncertain times.

Although Revelation spoke of the defeat of evil forces, it was never Christians who were the aggressors. John set up a comparison between the violence and aggressiveness of worldly behavior and the peace Christians embody. The instruction to Christians was not to rebel or wage war but to persevere and believe in God, trusting that He will make the burden lighter. It is a logical message to the early church. Christianity is still growing and far from being a major power in the world. The Roman Empire's military strength was unmatched, so encouraging Christians to fight would have been a death sentence. The Romans were surgical at stopping rebellions around the Empire. However, it was against the teachings of the faith to run and hide without proclaiming the truth. Therefore, Revelation is a reminder to be bold as well as an encouragement.

It was discouraging to have endured the pain the early Christians went through. John's visions highlight God's sovereignty so believers can trust that justice will come. Revelation speaks of plagues that will fall onto the nations, exploiting and killing Christians. Traditionally, plagues in the Bible facilitate repentance from evil nations. The nations would not repent, so Revelation explained how they would ultimately be destroyed.

Since the early church had little means to fight back, they had to accept the injustices forced on them daily. Hearing a message that justice would one day come was the hope they needed to live under the oppressive system without abandoning their faith. Revelation was written in a time of war when Jerusalem fell and the Roman Empire was in an expansionist mode. Considering their immense power, criticizing the Empire would not have been a smart choice for anyone. John had to veil his political criticisms so that if anyone found teaching or reading the text, they would not face the force of the Empire. One way to read Revelation is as prophecies for far into the future. However, early Christians likely understood it as a critique of the government and authorities while remaining hopeful that the wicked system would get what it deserved one day.

Christianity is an evangelical or missionary faith, meaning its doctrines encourage people to spread the message. Martyrdom was common in early Christianity because people openly preached a religion condemned by the authorities. Furthermore, they highlighted a heavenly King above the Emperor, who was meant to be viewed as a God by the Empire's citizens. Therefore, apocalyptic literature like Revelation gave early Christians a reason to keep holding onto their faith despite the clear negative consequences that were a pressing reality in their daily lives.

Themes of the Prophetic Book of Revelation

The first theme of the text is the corruption, opulence, greed, immorality, and wickedness of the ruling class. The personification of these vices and attitudes Revelation uses is the whore of Babylon. Babylon is the perfect description to address a Jewish audience or anyone familiar with the scripture. The evil and idolatry of Babylon were well-known among the audience of first-century Christians because it was a big part of the Israelite narrative concerning their judgment and redemption through Babylonian captivity. The imagery of a whore communicates recklessness and deep immorality. It links to the Old Testament symbology, where Israel was described as adulterous when they departed from God's ways.

Speech is a thematic focal point of Revelation. The image of Jesus returning with a tongue like a sword to destroy the evil nations highlights the power of speaking. John emphasizes the importance of spreading the message of the Gospel by talking about it. He understood that ideas spread through speech, and in the destitute position many Christians found themselves in, the only power they could use was their words. He highlights how Satan's kingdom uses the power of words to spread their propaganda and blasphemy.

Another core theme of Revelation is the anti-materialist views of Christianity. Through the communication of the vision he received, John emphasized the weakened faith of the church in Laodicea was tied to the wealth they obtained through exploitation, making them more accepting of Pagan ways. He reiterated the anti-materialist message by drawing parallels to Babylon and the Roman system obsessed with luxury. John realized that excessive wealth would lead people further from God. Therefore, Revelation encourages Christians to gain spiritual wealth instead of over-valuing worldly riches.

Revelation shows the difference between the messengers of Satan that lead to death and deceive the masses and compares that to the faithful followers or witnesses of Christ, who teach the truth to inherit abundant life. Therefore, as many of the epistles and Gospels emphasize, being aware of false teachers and doctrines that sound pleasing to the ear was essential. Christians should be rooted in their faith in Christ so that they cannot be swayed by the devil.

Revelation asserts that everyone worships something. The worship Revelation points believers to God and Christ, who laid down His life for the redemption of sinners. The other option of worship John put forth was of the beast or the dragon, representing the Roman or worldly system. However, worship of the latter would lead to destruction because deception is all they had to offer.

In the same lane as worship, Revelation often uses the symbology of a throne to show readers what they are submitting to. The throne of the evil authorities was set up to oppress people, which is why Christians should have worshipped the true King in Jesus Christ, who will help them prosper and bring liberation. The message of hope in Revelation is centered on God being above the powers of the world who oppressed the early Christians. Therefore, regardless of how Christians were tempted to deny their faith, the book encouraged them to trust in the One with true power, even above the Roman Emperors.

Activity 3

Choose a passage in Revelation and express the symbology and its meaning artistically. This can be a drawing, poem, song, or other artistic expression.

_____

_____

_____

_____

_____

_____

_____

_____

_____

_____

_____

_____

_____

_____

_____

_____

_____

_____

_____

_____

_____

_____

_____

_____

Section 10: Applying Biblical Principles: Lessons for Modern Life

Now that you've worked through all aspects of the scriptures, including the Mosaic Law, the wisdom literature, prophetic writings, Gospels, and epistles, you are ready to deeply consider how the Bible can be applied to your life. The scripture is not merely meant to be studied. Only one level of understanding emerges from the scholarly analysis of the text. You must apply the principles in a modern context to unfold the deeper layer.

The Biblical text contains timeless wisdom and principles that can enhance your life in multiple ways.[70]

It isn't easy to see how an ancient book can be relevant in a contemporary context. However, the Biblical text contains timeless wisdom and principles that can enhance your life in multiple ways. Furthermore, the Bible can take you from the material context to reveal profound spiritual truths transcending matter and time. To access this spiritual reality, you need to map the historical understanding of the scriptures onto your modern life to reveal the eternal truths.

The Bible is a lot more than just a book for believers. It is the text connecting you to a loving God and a Savior who sacrificed Himself for the forgiveness of your sins. You must walk through the principles of the Bible to comprehend the character of God and the role He plays in your life; then, you will understand why this sacrifice was necessary and the power behind it. This section of the workbook focuses on applying the Bible to bring you closer to God and grasp more profound spiritual mysteries embedded in the text. In this way, the Bible is not a cold and sterile book but transformed into a living scripture that unleashes an abundance of love, peace, and forgiveness in your everyday existence.

Key Biblical Principles and Themes

Although the Bible was written by many authors over the centuries, the miracle of the 66 books is that a consistent narrative managed to emerge. God's relationship with humanity is not as an aggressive tyrant who oppresses the masses but as a loving Father who guides His children through their rebellion, disobedience, and confusion. Hebrews 12:6 says, "The Lord disciplines the one he loves, and he chastens everyone he accepts as his son." This verse encapsulates why the Lord allowed many hardships to fall on his people. A loving parent does not discipline their child to hurt them but so they can learn a lesson, even though they may not understand.

God's wisdom is beyond the ways of humankind. People may never fully understand the motivations and functioning of the Lord in this life or the next. However, the spiritual journey increases your trust that you are complete in the hands of God. The human compulsion to control everything is deeply ingrained into the collective psyche. Understandably, when you feel in control, it creates security and safety. Spiritual practice is opening your tight fists that want to hold onto what is impossible to grab so you can relax into the open palms of letting go in the assurance that God knows what is best.

The revelation of Christ is realizing that of your strength alone, you can do nothing. Submitting to the will of God means following the Biblical principles He revealed an understanding that the love of God and faith in Him leads to abundant prosperity. Putting your life in the hands of God does not mean you sit idly back and do nothing. It is the opposite because it means all your decisions are made by considering what God would want you to do. When you fail to align to Godly principles and stumble, you will commit to turning back to the Lord continuously, living a life of repentance, and demonstrating your faith in Christ through your work.

Love

The Bible says that God is Love. This is a profound statement because it goes beyond saying that God has or possesses love. It describes love as the essence of the Lord. If God is love, then His actions and interactions with humanity must be viewed through this lens. By the extended Biblical narrative through the scriptures, God demonstrates that His love is selfless and unfaltering. When the disciples asked Jesus what the greatest of all the commandments were, the Messiah replied in Mark 12:30-31, "Love the Lord your God with all your heart and with all your soul and with all your mind and with all your strength. The second is this: 'Love your neighbor as yourself.' There is no commandment greater than these." This shows that love is the central component of faith. As God loves unconditionally, humankind created in His image should show the same love to each other.

The heart of humanity has turned to wickedness, meaning it is filled with hate. Hence, it is so easy to envy, bad-mouth, and embrace selfishness. However, through submitting to Christ, your stone heart is turned into a heart of flesh. The more you gear yourself toward loving God, the more your love for your neighbors and enemies will shine through. The key to self-actualization is selflessly loving as the Messiah did when He died on the cross for your sins. Amid torture, Jesus pleas for God's mercy on the perpetrators because, in His divinity, He understood the actions were ill-informed. This is the standard of love a believer should pursue – that even those who plan to harm you should receive nothing but love from you.

This unwavering love is difficult to achieve. Therefore, spiritual transformation takes consistent effort. A good way to understand it is if you take one step toward God, He will take three toward you. When you practice love consistently through your words, thoughts, and deeds, God will multiply this spirit in you. However, when you consciously and continuously slip into selfishness, God will multiply the same spirit in you. The beauty of the Lord is that His arms are always open, and you can turn to Him no matter how far you've fallen.

Forgiveness and Mercy

Humans are not perfect. Since the fall of Adam and Eve in the Garden of Eden, humanity has turned toward a wicked nature. God's relationship with the Israelites in the Old Testament shows that although His righteous judgment must take place, in His infinite mercy, He always made a plan for His people to be redeemed and turn back to Him. This merciful and forgiving nature culminates in the incarnation, death, and resurrection of Christ.

The imagery of a marriage describes God's relationship with humanity. The church is called the Bride of Christ (Ephesians 5: 22-23). Similar symbolism was used for the Israelites in the Old Testament. God highlights how His people are like adulterous brides because they embrace wickedness and idolatry. However, God is faithful, so He always creates a plan for redemption. By sacrificing His son, according to the Christian understanding, God has paid the final price for humankind to find a pathway back to Him, which is why the Bible asserts that no one goes to the Father except through Christ.

As the image of God, humanity should reflect His forgiving nature. The Lord's Prayer says He should forgive us as we forgive those who trespass against us. So, God expects humanity to show mercy to one another. Christ taught this lesson practically when the people wanted to stone the adulterous woman according to the Mosaic law, but Jesus said that whoever has no sin should be the first one to cast a stone (John 8 7-11). Another analogy Christ uses is that before you remove the splinter from your brother's eye, you should remove the log from your own. Essentially, the Bible teaches that you should recognize your imperfections and that you require forgiveness to freely forgive others.

Justice

God is merciful, but He is also just. Therefore, every sin which is committed against Him must be punished. The crucifixion can be understood as a balance between God's mercy and His justice. Imagine you are before God in a court case. The prosecutor reads out all your sins, and your sentence is announced. God, as the judge says, although you are guilty, someone has already paid your fine, so you are free to go. The death of Christ represents the payment of the debt sin creates.

Embodying Biblical justice in your life means you should not focus on vengeance when someone wrongs you but leave a path for forgiveness and mercy. If you weigh yourself on the scale of justice and trace how many people you have wronged and, more importantly, how often you have sinned against God, the mercy He shows by allowing you to breathe is unmatched. As much as God judged the nations, including Israel, in the scriptures, there was always an opportunity for redemption.

The Bible describes that the Lord is slow to anger, so when His wrathful justice eventually appeared, it was after a long time of providing opportunities for people to adjust their actions. Similarly, if you reflect the spirit of God, your anger should not be reckless and uncontrolled. Emotions are human, and you will lose your temper. However, as a faithful believer, you cannot allow your emotions to control you and should always strive to align your conduct with the patient nature of the Lord.

Faithfulness and God's Sovereignty

You may have achieved something great in your life. You look at your achievements and believe it is your hard work that got you there. However, at any second, it could all be taken away in a multitude of ways that are out of your control. Faith is realizing that everything about your life is in God's hands. Increasing your faith means trusting in the Lord.

In the Christian worldview, it is not your deeds that save you but faith in Christ because faith in a sovereign God puts Him as the focus. God has plans to prosper you, so the hardships you experience are for your benefit in this life or eternity. Therefore, your trust in the Lord should remain solid. Faith in Christ is what justifies you before God. Your works will become righteous not because of your effort but because your belief propels you through a transformation of the heart.

Faith is when you rely wholly on God. When the Israelites were in the desert, they wanted to return to Egypt at some point because, at least in captivity, they knew what to expect. However, they did not realize that belief in the unseen and trust in God, who constantly provided, was greater because ahead was the Promised Land. Merely because it is not in front of your eyes does not mean it is not real. Trusting the Lord even in adversity is a central teaching of the Bible. It can be applied in your life when your back is against the wall – and you have no choice but to turn to the Creator. The Lord sometimes puts people in uncomfortable positions so they can turn back to Him.

How These Principles Fit into the Modern World

The selfless love encouraged by the Bible is needed more now than ever. Every doctrine of the world preaches self-love, self-development, and self-image, meaning selfishness has become a core value in society. Social media enhances this as people constantly promote their ideas, compete for attention, and try to outshine the next person. The love of Christ is selfless. The New Testament teaches that you should love your brother more than yourself. This is almost unimaginable in a modern world that considers this boundless love as *self-destructive.*

Applying the principles of the Bible in the contemporary era means catering to God first.[71]

Applying the principles of the Bible in the contemporary era means catering to God first and letting His love exude from your life. As you place God as the focal point, your will is diminished, and His will takes over. The world preaches to find yourself, but the Bible preaches to deny yourself. As you submit fully to God, your perception will be radically transformed. Instead of solely wondering how your actions and the deeds of others affect you, you will consider those around you and realize they are as worthy of love as you are.

Embracing Biblical principles in the modern world is a revolutionary act. As Jesus condemned many of the Jewish leaders in the Old Testament because they had lost the spirit of the law, unfortunately, many church leaders are on the same path. It makes no sense that a preacher has excessive wealth and sits among celebrities while people in his congregation suffer. Embracing the spirit of God through the Bible's teachings means alienation in many cases, but like the early church, which suffered persecution, an abundance of light and spiritual transformation is a reward for your steadfastness in the faith.

Personalizing the Bible to Your Life

Personal

Humans are social creatures. So, in essence, your personal life comprises relationships, including friendships, family, and romantic bonds. Scriptures teach selfless love, so this is the core value that should permeate your relationships. Love should be the driving force of how you conduct yourself in your relationships. The love God shows you is what you should put out into the world. Being forgiving, patient, slow to anger, selfless, and encouraging should replace mindlessly tearing each other down. The world promotes competition and envy, but Biblically, collaboration is the guide because scripture commands you to love your neighbor as yourself.

Professional

The Wisdom literature teaches the importance of hard work. A lazy person is not likely to earn as much as a hard worker. So, in your professional life, it is advisable to give your all. However, the Wisdom teachings are based on probability. Therefore, working hard is not a guarantee you will get wealth. Doing the best you can but recognizing it is all in God's hands is how you acknowledge the Lord's sovereignty in your professional life.

The central teaching of the scriptures, which is love for God and your fellow man, should come forward in your workplace. This doesn't mean you should be preaching when it is time for work, but at the lunch table, some evangelism could be helpful if you are a believer. Furthermore, spreading love in your conduct with your colleagues is how you build Biblical professional relationships. Back-biting and snakish attitudes are not what Scripture teaches. Remember, the economic system is in the control of the devil, so it is easy to fall into wicked ways at work. Staying focused on God and relying on His guidance lets you manifest His righteousness, mercy, and love in the workplace.

Honest conduct as a professional is essential. The judgment for exploitation in the Bible is harsh. If you have a business or work for someone, remember the Lord does not look kindly on those who take advantage of others. As much as you need to make money to survive in the world, you should not be so focused on luxury and material possessions that it erodes your moral character. Christ taught that it is easier for a wealthy person to go through a needle's eye than it is to get into heaven. This was not a condemnation of wealth but a warning that materialism can easily corrupt you. A Christian should work to live - not live to work - because then your profession becomes an idol.

Societal

Society is built on Darwinian principles of survival of the fittest. The myth of meritocracy has been shattered, and an increasing number of people are becoming disillusioned with the world's system. The Bible calls Satan the god of this age and ruler of the world. That does not mean Satan is equivalent to God. It also does not refer to Satan sharing in God's power as the creator of the universe. However, it highlights the reality that the institutions and structures of the world have fallen into evil, including the media, education, governments, and the economy.

Think of a simple item like your smartphone. Thousands of people were exploited to create that product. The conditions of the mines where people work for the materials are dangerous, and they are underpaid. Many of the factories that assemble and build phones are also exploitative. A similar route of oppression can be traced to almost every product you own. Therefore, the structures of the world are wicked. The Old Testament nations received the most judgment when they mistreated the vulnerable. In the global economic market, the poor are the most vulnerable, and the system falls apart without their exploitation.

Acting as a Christian should societally require you to uplift the vulnerable like the poor, orphans, drug addicts, and exploited of the world. Therefore, your actions and advocacy should be geared toward ensuring those who need love the most are cared for. You cannot single-handedly change society and shift the evil functioning of the world, but it does not mean you should remain stagnant. Jesus said with faith, the size of a mustard seed, you can move mountains (Matthew 17: 20-21), so it is important to remember the transformative power embedded in you as long as you cleave to the will of the Most High.

Activity

Reflect on the themes and principles in the Bible. Highlight some key teachings. Write about how you can apply these principles in the various areas of your life, including family, finance, relationships, and anything else you wish to include. Think about your triumphs and struggles and how you can use Biblical principles to navigate these complexities.

Conclusion

Now that you have worked through this activity book, the Bible has been demystified. You have the foundational knowledge to excel in continually discovering scripture's truth. Not every lesson may have resonated with you now, but as life evolves, you will see some parts of the book become more relevant when you revisit them. Therefore, feel free to work through the exercises as often as needed and review the theoretical explanations as your knowledge deepens.

Studying the Bible is not a once-off activity. The living text reveals new layers the more you explore it. This workbook is like a launching pad off which you can be blasted into new territories. Exploring becomes easier when you know where to look and have a map. However, it is only on the journey that you truly unlock the full capabilities of the adventure. The difference between reading the Bible and living its principles is like looking at a natural wonder on television or in a picture and seeing it in real life. If you saw a photo, you might be able to describe it in detail, but when you are in the middle of a miracle, you experience it and are profoundly transformed.

This book was crafted to tie the scholarly view of the Bible with the practical and spiritual aspects of the text. The difference between knowledge and wisdom is experience. You can read a million books about the details of heart surgery, but you'll never gain the expertise unless you get on the surgery floor and begin operating. The same applies to dissecting the Bible. Some of the most profound lessons are only found by putting the work into practice.

Although you are at the end of this book, you are only starting your journey. People have dedicated their lives to studying and living the scriptures. As you follow the threads woven into these practical activities, your path continues further into new wonders. God is perfect, and as you study the Bible to get closer to God, you will travel the lifelong journey of perfecting yourself through the grace of Christ. This book is a tool to help strengthen your relationship with the Most High and help you follow Biblical principles under the sovereign guidance of the Lord. The Lord's justice, mercy, and grace govern all, so by connecting to His power through the study and application of scripture, you can rest in the loving palms of God.

If you enjoyed this book, a review on Amazon would be greatly appreciated because it would mean a lot to hear from you.

To leave a review:

1. Open your camera app.
2. Point your mobile device at the QR code.
3. The review page will appear in your web browser.

_____

Thanks for your support!

Check out another book in the series

Welcome Aboard, Check Out This Limited-Time Free Bonus!

Ahoy, reader! Welcome to the Ahoy Publications family, and thanks for snagging a copy of this book! Since you've chosen to join us on this journey, we'd like to offer you something special.

Check out the link below for a **FREE** e-book filled with delightful facts about American History.

But that's not all - you'll also have access to our exclusive email list with even more free e-books and insider knowledge. Well, what are ye waiting for? Click the link below to join and set sail toward exciting adventures in American History.

Access your bonus here
https://ahoypublications.com/
Or, Scan the QR code!

References

Adam and Eve in the Garden of Eden - Bible Story. (2020, October 12). Bible Study Tools; Salem Web Network. https://www.Biblestudytools.com/Bible-stories/adam-and-eve-in-the-garden.html

Bible Summary - Genesis. (n.d.). Biblesummary.Info. https://Biblesummary.info/genesis

Guzik, D. (2015, June 19). Enduring Word Bible Commentary Genesis Chapter 1. Enduring Word. https://enduringword.com/Bible-commentary/genesis-1/

Duncan, L. (2001, April 1). The Third and Fourth Plagues: Gnats and Flies. Reformed Theological Seminary. https://rts.edu/resources/the-third-and-fourth-plagues-gnats-and-flies/

The Tenth Plague: the Sound of the Final Note. (n.d.). Reformedfellowship.net. https://outlook.reformedfellowship.net/sermons/the-tenth-plague-the-sound-of-the-final-note/?hilite=tenth+plague

What Was the Meaning and Purpose of the Ten Plagues of Egypt? (2013, December 31). Gotquestions.org. https://www.gotquestions.org/ten-plagues-Egypt.html

Hu, W. (2012). Unsupervised Learning of Two Bible Books: Proverbs and Psalms. Sociology Mind, 02(03), 325–334. https://doi.org/10.4236/sm.2012.23043

Mcleod, J. (2010, September 27). Wisdom in Adversity. Sermon Central. https://www.sermoncentral.com/sermons/wisdom-in-adversity-jonathan-mcleod-sermon-on-wisdom-150400

Psalms. (n.d.). Insight.org. https://insight.org/resources/ Bible/the-wisdom-books/psalms

Psalms Versus Proverbs Compare and Contrast - Free Comparison Essay Example, Compare and Contrast Paper. (2020, June 2). StudyMoose. https://studymoose.com/psalms-verses-proverbs-compare-contrast-new-essay

Turning Point. (2020, January 15). 15 Benefits to Reading Psalms and Proverbs. David Jeremiah Blog. https://davidjeremiah.blog/15-benefits-to-reading-psalms-and-proverbs/

Davisson, M. (2023, February 22). A Life-Changing Encounter for the Woman with the Issue of Blood. Cups to Crowns. https://www.cupstocrowns.com/blog/woman-with-issue-of-blood

Life of Christ - Events, Miracles, Teachings, and Purpose. (2015, April 17). NeverThirsty; Like the Master Ministries. https://www.neverthirsty.org/about-christ/life-of-christ/

The Life of Jesus: A Chronological Study. (n.d.). FaithGateway Store. https://faithgateway.com/blogs/christian-books/life-of-jesus-chronological-study

The Parable of the Sower of Seed - The Kingdom of God - Ccea - Gcse Religious Studies Revision - CCEA. (n.d.). BBC. https://www.bbc.co.uk/bitesize/guides/zd76rj6/revision/2

Understanding the Good Samaritan Parable. (2023, December 27). Biblical Archaeology Society. https://www.biblicalarchaeology.org/daily/archaeology-today/archaeologists-biblical-scholars-works/understanding-the-good-samaritan-parable/

What Is the Meaning of the Story of the Woman with the Issue of Blood? (2013, September 4). Gotquestions.org. https://www.gotquestions.org/woman-issue-blood.html

Aaron. (2017, February 22). Acts 10: Understanding the Meaning of Peter's Vision –. Path of Obedience. https://www.pathofobedience.com/scripture/acts/understanding-peters-vision/

Anderson, D. (2015, November 13). What Acts Teaches Us about Advancing the Gospel. Open the Bible. https://opentheBible.org/article/what-acts-teaches-us-about-advancing-the-gospel/

Carter, E. (n.d.). Acts: Lessons from the Early Church. Fervr.net. https://fervr.net/ Bible/acts-lessons-from-the-early-church

Ministries, R. (2024, February 22). Daily Devotional Library —. Today's Daily Devotional. https://todaydevotional.com/daily-devotional-library

Study 7 The Meaning of Pentecost. (2013, April 6). Words of Life Ministries CIO. https://www.wordsoflife.co.uk/ Bible-studies/study-7-the-meaning-of-pentecost/

Introduction to Colossians. (n.d.). ESV Bible. https://www.esv.org/resources/esv-global-study- Bible/introduction-to-colossians/

Ma, C. (2021, May 18). What is The Book of Romans About? Alabaster Co. https://www.alabasterco.com/blogs/education/what-is-the-book-of-romans-about

Willems, K. (2017, April 8). Who was the Apostle Paul? - a Brief Biography (what he did and wrote) —. Kurt Willems. https://www.kurtwillems.com/blog/apostle-paul-brief-biography

Ephesus - The Loveless Church. (n.d.). Lineage Journey. https://lineagejourney.com/read/ephesus-the-loveless-church/

Guthrie, N. (2022, May 11). 10 Things You Should Know about the Book of Revelation. Crossway. https://www.crossway.org/articles/10-things-you-should-know-about-the-book-of-revelation/

Hall, E. (1992). Revelation. Journal for the Study of the New Testament, 15, 125–125. https://doi.org/10.1177/0142064x9201504814

Laodicea — The Lukewarm Church Is Neither Hot nor Cold. (2020, August 23). NeverThirsty; Like the Master Ministries. https://www.neverthirsty.org/ Bible-studies/evaluating-health-your-church/the-lukewarm-church-is-neither-hot-nor-cold/

Pergamos: The Compromised Church. (n.d.). Lineage Journey. https://lineagejourney.com/read/pergamos-the-compromised-church/

Revelation, Apocalypse, John, Patmos, Nero, Domitian. (n.d.). Ccel.org. https://www.ccel.org/ Bible/phillips/CPn27Revelation.htm

Townsend, A., Doubiago, S., Laux, D., & Scates, M. (1991). Books of Revelation. 8, 34. https://doi.org/10.2307/4021065

What does Revelation 1:20 Mean? (n.d.). Bibleref.com. https://www.Bibleref.com/Revelation/1/Revelation-1-20.html

(N.d.). Godversusreligion.com. https://godversusreligion.com/the-letter-to-the-corrupt-church-in-thyatira-revelation/

az Bible.com. (n.d.). List of Bible Prophets. Az Bible.com. https://www.az Bible.com/prophets-in-the- Bible.html

Kranz, J. (2019, October 3). The Beginner's Guide to the Prophets in the Bible.Overview Bible. https://overviewBible.com/prophets/

Talk, F. (2023, November 15). The Prophets of the Old Testament. Hopelify Media - Share The Good News. Christian. Hopeful. Relevant. https://hopelify.org/the-prophets-of-the-old-testament/

Theology of Work. (2012, September 29). Introduction to the Prophets. Theology of Work. https://www.theologyofwork.org/old-testament/introduction-to-the-prophets/

Fairchild, M. (2011, January 28). Historical Books. Learn Religions. https://www.learnreligions.com/historical-books-of-the- Bible-700269

Howard, D. M. (2022, December 21). Introduction to the Old Testament Historical Books. The Gospel Coalition. https://www.thegospelcoalition.org/essay/historical-books/

IF:Gathering. (2021, April 26). IF:Gathering. https://www.ifgathering.com/ifequip/studies/how-to-read-your- Bible/the-historical-books-of-the-old-testament/

The Historical Books in the Old Testament. (2021, January 1). Churchofjesuschrist.org. https://www.churchofjesuschrist.org/study/manual/come-follow-me-for-individuals-and-families-old-testament-2022/22-thoughts?lang=eng

The Old Testament Historical Books (Joshua through Esther): An outline. (n.d.). Bible.org. https://Bible.org/series/old-testament-historical-books-joshua-through-esther-outline

Connecting the Old & New Testament —. (n.d.). The Chara Project. https://www.thecharaproject.com/old-and-new-testament

Old and New Testament Connection. (n.d.). Bibleone.net. http://Bibleone.net/Old-and-New-Testament-Connection.htm

Schrock, D. (2020, September 10). The Relation of the Old and New Testaments. The Gospel Coalition. https://www.thegospelcoalition.org/essay/the-relation-of-the-old-and-new-testaments/

Theology of Work. (2013, December 6). Discovering a Link between the Old and New Testaments. Theology of Work. https://www.theologyofwork.org/the-high-calling/discovering-link-between-old-and-new-testaments/

Kapp, Tristán. (2020). Towards a promised land: Tracing the origins of Israel and the Colonization of Canaan from Joshua 1-12 to Judges 1-2. 10.13140/RG.2.2.16111.87209.

Let There Be God: How Yahweh became "God Almighty." (2022, June 22). Big Think. https://bigthink.com/the-past/yahweh-god-origins-israel/

Norman, J. (n.d.). The Gezer Calendar, One of the Earliest Surviving Examples of Written Hebrew: History of Information. Historyofinformation.com. https://www.historyofinformation.com/detail.php?id=1280

Smith, M. S. (2004). The Memoirs of God: History, Memory, and the Experience of the Divine in Ancient Israel. Fortress Press.

Smith, M. S., & Miller, P. D. (2002). The Early History of God: Yahweh and the other deities in ancient Israel. William B. Eerdmans Publishing Company.

What Was the Significance of the Commands Against Mixing Different Things in Deuteronomy 22:9–11? (n.d.). GotQuestions.org. https://www.gotquestions.org/commands-against-mixing.html

New International Version. (2011). BibleGateway.com. http://www.biblegateway.com/versions/

qdroach. (2013, March 21). Another Reason to Learn the Bible's Overarching Story. BibleMesh. https://biblemesh.com/blog/another-reason-to-learn-the-bibles-overarching-story/

Isaacs, R. H. (n.d.). A Summary of the Torah. My Jewish Learning. https://www.myjewishlearning.com/article/a-summary-of-the-torah/

Ondich, J. (2022). The Torah. Minnstate.pressbooks.pub. https://minnstate.pressbooks.pub/bible/part/the-torah/

Vaillancourt, I. J. (2022, November 6). 10 Things You Should Know about the Pentateuch. Crossway. https://www.crossway.org/articles/10-things-you-should-know-about-the-pentateuch/

Berger, B. (2019, December 5). Theology Thursday: What Are the Biblical Covenants? GCU. https://www.gcu.edu/blog/theology-ministry/theology-thursday-what-are-biblical-covenants

George, J. (2023, June 22). Literary Structure of the Bible: Old and New Testament Books. Christianity.com. https://www.christianity.com/wiki/bible/literary-structure-of-the-bible-11528149.html

Quick Summary - Bible History. (n.d.). Bible-History.com. https://bible-history.com/old-testament/quicksummary

Schochet, D. (n.d.). The Story of King David in the Bible. Chabad.org. https://www.chabad.org/library/article_cdo/aid/520477/jewish/The-Story-of-King-David-in-the-Bible.htm#Davids

Your Adventist Friend. (2022, April 29). Who Were the Judges of Israel in the Old Testament? AskAnAdventistFriend.com. https://www.askanadventistfriend.com/understanding-the-bible/old-testament/judges-of-israel/

An Introduction to the Book of Proverbs | Bible.org. (n.d.). Bible.org. https://bible.org/article/introduction-book-proverbs

Book of Proverbs - Read, Study Bible Verses Online. (n.d.). Bible Study Tools. https://www.biblestudytools.com/proverbs/

Book of Proverbs Overview - Insight for Living Ministries. (n.d.). Insight.org. https://insight.org/resources/bible/the-wisdom-books/proverbs

Gaiser, F. (n.d.). Summary of Psalms. Enter the Bible. https://enterthebible.org/courses/psalms/lessons/summary-of-psalms

Guide to the Book of Psalms: Key Information and Helpful Resources. (n.d.). BibleProject. https://bibleproject.com/guides/book-of-psalms/

Limburg, J. (n.d.). Theological Themes in Proverbs. Enter the Bible. https://enterthebible.org/courses/proverbs/lessons/theological-themes-in-proverbs

Main Themes of Ecclesiastes | Water on Thirsty Land. (2021, May 19). Water on Thirsty Land. https://www.wateronthirstyland.com/ecclesiastes-bible-book-overview/

Parables in the Old Testament – Bible History. (n.d.). Bible-History.com. https://bible-history.com/old-testament/parables

Summary of the Book of Psalms – Bible Survey. (n.d.). GotQuestions.org. https://www.gotquestions.org/Book-of-Psalms.html

The Parables of the Old Testament. (2019, February 20). Livingwithfaith.org. http://www.livingwithfaith.org/blog/the-parables-of-the-old-testament

What Is the Background of Proverbs? (n.d.). Bibles.net. https://www.bibles.net/book-background/background-of-proverbs/

Baxter, M. (1988). The Formation of the Christian Scriptures. Westminster John Knox Press. Cline, A. (2019, June 25). Three Synoptic Gospels – Compare and Contrast. Learn Religions. https://www.learnreligions.com/synoptic-gospel-problem-248782

Ford, C. (n.d.). Christological Controversies in the Early Church. The Gospel Coalition. https://www.thegospelcoalition.org/essay/christological-controversies-in-the-early-church/

Long, K. (2022, September 8). The Synoptic Gospels Compared to the Gospel of John. Bart D. Ehrman – New Testament Scholar, Speaker, and Consultant. https://www.bartehrman.com/the-synoptic-gospels/

Mackie, T., & Sullivan, A. (2017, May 26). Old Rituals & New Realities: The Day of Atonement and Jesus' Death. BibleProject. https://bibleproject.com/articles/old-rituals-new-realities/

Orr, P. (2023, January 10). What Is Distinct about the Theology of Mark? Crossway. https://www.crossway.org/articles/what-is-distinct-about-the-theology-of-mark/

Parton, C. (2012, November 9). Why Did the Early Christians Reject the "Alternative Gospels"? Exploring the Faith. https://exploringthefaith.com/2012/11/09/alternative-gospels/

BibleStudyTools Staff. (2019, January 23). Paul in the Bible. Bible Study Tools; Salem Web Network. https://www.biblestudytools.com/topical-verses/paul-in-the-bible/

Curtis, D. B. (2008, March 30). From Jerusalem to Rome – Acts 1:6-8: Berean Bible Church. Www.bereanbiblechurch.org. https://www.bereanbiblechurch.org/transcripts/acts/1_6-8.htm

Fairchild, M. (2019, May 6). Discover What the Bible's Book of Acts Is All About. Learn Religions. https://www.learnreligions.com/book-of-acts-701031

Henrich, S. (n.d.). Background of Acts. Enter the Bible. https://enterthebible.org/courses/acts/lessons/background-of-acts

Jakes, M. (2023, March 10). Who Wrote the Book of Acts? Biblestudytools.com. https://www.biblestudytools.com/bible-study/topical-studies/who-wrote-the-book-of-acts.html

Nelson, R. (2019, March 29). Who Was Saint Luke? The Beginner's Guide. OverviewBible. https://overviewbible.com/saint-luke/

Stam, K. (2014). Acts 6:7 – The Growing Word | Christian Library. Christianstudylibrary.org. https://www.christianstudylibrary.org/article/acts-67-%E2%80%93-growing-word

Vickers, B. (2019, September 30). What Are the Tongues of Fire? (Acts 2). Crossway. https://www.crossway.org/articles/what-are-the-tongues-of-fire-acts-2/

What "Catholic" Means. (2018, November 19). Catholic Answers. https://www.catholic.com/tract/what-catholic-means

What is the Day of Pentecost? (n.d.). GotQuestions.org. https://www.gotquestions.org/day-Pentecost.html

What is the Meaning/Definition of the Word Catholic? | GotQuestions.org. (2010, November 13). GotQuestions.org. https://www.gotquestions.org/Catholic-meaning-definition.html

Who was Paul in the Bible? (2009, December 12). GotQuestions.org. https://www.gotquestions.org/life-Paul.html

Why was Paul in Prison? (n.d.). GotQuestions.org. https://www.gotquestions.org/why-was-Paul-in-prison.html

A Quick Guide to the Pauline Epistles | OverviewBible. (2018). OverviewBible. https://overviewbible.com/pauline-epistles/Book of Hebrews | Guide with Key Information and Resources. (n.d.). BibleProject. https://bibleproject.com/guides/book-of-hebrews/

Deutero-Pauline Book. (n.d.). Enter the Bible. https://enterthebible.org/glossary/deutero-pauline-book

Ehrman, B. D. (2009). A Brief Introduction to the New Testament. Oxford University Press, USA.GotQuestions.org. (2006, May 16). Who wrote the Book of Hebrews? Who was the author of Hebrews? | GotQuestions.org. GotQuestions.org. https://www.gotquestions.org/author-Hebrews.html

Guzik, D. (2015, December 7). Enduring Word Bible Commentary 2 Thessalonians Chapter 2. Enduring Word. https://enduringword.com/bible-commentary/2-thessalonians-2/

Hultgren, A. J. (n.d.). Introductory Issues in 1 Timothy. Enter the Bible. https://enterthebible.org/courses/1-timothy/lessons/introductory-issues-in-1-timothy

Jude – Bible Book Chapters and Summary – New International Version. (n.d.). Www.christianity.com. https://www.christianity.com/bible/niv/jude/

Just, F. (n.d.). Deutero-Pauline Letters. Catholic-Resources.org. https://catholic-resources.org/Bible/Paul-Disputed.htm

Just, F. (n.d.). Epistles of Peter. Catholic-Resources.org. https://catholic-resources.org/Bible/Epistles-Peter.htm

O'Neal, S. (2018, July 22). Examination of the Pauline Epistles. Learn Religions. https://www.learnreligions.com/overview-the-epistles-of-the-new-testament-363407

Summary of the Book of 1 Corinthians – Bible Survey. (n.d.). GotQuestions.org. https://www.gotquestions.org/Book-of-1-Corinthians.html

Summary of the Book of 2 Timothy – Bible Survey. (n.d.). GotQuestions.org. https://www.gotquestions.org/Book-of-2-Timothy.html

Summary of the Book of Ephesians – Bible Survey. (n.d.). GotQuestions.org. https://www.gotquestions.org/Book-of-Ephesians.html

Summary of the Book of Galatians – Bible Survey. (n.d.). GotQuestions.org. https://www.gotquestions.org/Book-of-Galatians.html

Swindoll, C. (n.d.). Book of First Thessalonians Overview – Insight for Living Ministries. Insight.org. https://insight.org/resources/bible/the-pauline-epistles/first-thessalonians

Swindoll, C. (n.d.). Book of James Overview – Insight for Living Ministries. Insight.org. https://insight.org/resources/bible/the-general-epistles/james

Swindoll, C. (2020). Book of Second Corinthians Overview – Insight for Living Ministries. Insight.org. https://insight.org/resources/bible/the-pauline-epistles/second-corinthians

Theology of Work. (n.d.). Summary & Conclusion to Romans. Theology of Work. https://www.theologyofwork.org/new-testament/romans-and-work/conclusions-romans/

Theology of Work. (n.d.). The Pastoral Epistles and Work. Theology of Work. https://www.theologyofwork.org/new-testament/pastoral-epistles/

What are the General Epistles? (n.d.). GotQuestions.org. https://www.gotquestions.org/general-epistles.html

Whittaker, J. (2022, August 2). Summary of Colossians: Understanding the Basics of Colossians in the Bible. Renew.org. https://renew.org/summary-of-colossians-understanding-the-basics-of-colossians-in-the-bible/

Who was Philemon in the Bible? (n.d.). GotQuestions.org. https://www.gotquestions.org/Philemon-in-the-Bible.html

Koester, C. R. (n.d.). Summary of Revelation. Enter the Bible. https://enterthebible.org/courses/revelation/lessons/summary-of-revelation

Pagels, E. (2012, March 7). Book Of Revelation: "Visions, Prophecy, And Politics." Npr.org. https://www.npr.org/2012/03/07/148125942/the-book-of-revelation-visions-prophecy-politics

Revelation: It's No Mystery. (n.d.). GCI Archive. https://archive.gci.org/articles/revelation-its-no-mystery/

White, L. M. (n.d.). Book Of Revelation | Apocalypse! FRONTLINE | PBS. Www.pbs.org. https://www.pbs.org/wgbh/pages/frontline/shows/apocalypse/revelation/white.html

Are we supposed to let go and let God? (n.d.). GotQuestions.org. https://www.gotquestions.org/let-go-and-let-God.html

Grace Theological Seminary. (2022, May 27). What does faith mean? Grace Theological Seminary. https://seminary.grace.edu/what-does-faith-mean/

Hanegraaff, H. (2023, May 2). Why is Satan called "the god of this age"? Christian Research Institute. https://www.equip.org/bible_answers/why-is-satan-called-the-god-of-this-age/

Love in the Bible | Resource Guide | BibleProjectTM. (n.d.). BibleProject. https://bibleproject.com/guides/love-in-the-bible/

Theology of Work. (n.d.). 10 Key Points About Work in the Bible Every Christian Should Know. Theology of Work. https://www.theologyofwork.org/resources/what-does-the-bible-say-about-work/

Image Sources

[1] *https://www.pexels.com/photo/close-up-photo-of-Bible-4654082/*

[2] *https://www.pexels.com/photo/sun-eclipse-9647389/*

[3] *https://www.pexels.com/photo/monochrome-photo-of-flock-of-flying-birds-1386454/*

[4] *https://www.flickr.com/photos/44534236@N00/16895519109*

[5] *https://www.pexels.com/photo/close-up-shot-of-Bible-verse-5025563/*

[6] *https://www.flickr.com/photos/paullew/9304183235*

[7] *https://www.pexels.com/photo/ancient-temple-by-the-river-in-egypt-18934581/*

[8] *Philip De Vere, CC BY-SA 3.0 <https://creativecommons.org/licenses/by-sa/3.0>, via Wikimedia Commons. https://commons.wikimedia.org/wiki/File:The_Phillip_Medhurst_Picture_Torah_345._The_plague_of_locusts._Exodus_cap_10_vv_13-15._Jan_Luyken.jpg*

[9] *See page for author, CC0, via Wikimedia Commons. https://commons.wikimedia.org/wiki/File:The_Sacred_Books_and_Early_Literature_of_the_East,_vol._2,_pg._208-209,_Anubis.jpg*

[10] *https://www.pexels.com/photo/text-on-a-white-paper-11506033/*

[11] *https://www.pexels.com/photo/close-up-shot-of-book-of-proverbs-11877603/*

[12] *https://unsplash.com/photos/man-kneeling-down-near-shore-bEbqpPeHEM4*

[13] *https://www.pexels.com/photo/delicious-honeycomb-filled-with-honey-8105066/*

[14] *https://www.pexels.com/photo/holy-family-figurines-6244101/*

[15] *https://www.flickr.com/photos/paullew/48112995663*

[16] *https://www.pexels.com/photo/wine-glass-with-red-wine-391213/*

[17] *https://www.pexels.com/photo/crucifix-illustration-208216/*

[18] *https://www.pexels.com/photo/man-and-people-in-jesus-christ-and-apostles-costumes-8958075/*

[19] https://www.pexels.com/photo/newtestament-book-2565227/

[20] Dnalor 01, CC BY-SA 3.0 AT <https://creativecommons.org/licenses/by-sa/3.0/at/deed.en>, via Wikimedia Commons. https://commons.wikimedia.org/wiki/File:Rom,_Vatikan,_Basilika_St._Peter,_Die_Taube_des_Heiligen_Geistes_(Cathedra_Petri,_Bernini).jpg

[21] https://www.flickr.com/photos/paullew/7203069100

[22] https://commons.wikimedia.org/wiki/File:Bartolomeo_Montagna_-_Saint_Paul_-_Google_Art_Project.jpg

[23] https://commons.wikimedia.org/wiki/File:Rembrandt_-_Apostle_Paul_-_WGA19120.jpg

[24] https://commons.wikimedia.org/wiki/File:Lavinia_Fontana_Christ_and_the_Samaritan_Woman_at_the_Well.jpg

[25] https://www.pexels.com/photo/person-writing-on-white-paper-6860815/

[26] cjh1452000, CC0, via Wikimedia Commons. https://commons.wikimedia.org/wiki/File:Nero-black.png

[27] Rodhullandemu, CC BY-SA 4.0 <https://creativecommons.org/licenses/by-sa/4.0>, via Wikimedia Commons. https://commons.wikimedia.org/wiki/File:15_Angel_with_long_trumpet_window,_St_Nicholas,_Halewood.jpg

[28] https://www.pexels.com/photo/the-old-testament-in-the-Bible-2565226/

[29] https://www.pexels.com/photo/a-book-with-a-page-open-to-a-page-with-text-19030919/

[30] https://www.pexels.com/search/Zephaniah/

[31] https://www.pexels.com/photo/paintings-on-the-church-indoor-walls-8349022/

[32] https://www.pexels.com/photo/texts-on-a-Bible-in-close-up-photography-6241862/

[33] https://www.pexels.com/photo/grayscale-photo-of-a-person-reading-a-Bible-5206035/

[34] https://www.pexels.com/photo/a-person-holding-a-Bible-5199801/

[35] https://www.pexels.com/photo/jesus-christ-stained-glass-46154/

[36] LMP 2001, CC BY-SA 4.0 <https://creativecommons.org/licenses/by-sa/4.0>, via Wikimedia Commons. https://commons.wikimedia.org/wiki/File:Holy_Spirit_Manila_Cathedral_2024-05-19.jpg

[37] NYC Wanderer (Kevin Eng), CC BY-SA 2.0 <https://creativecommons.org/licenses/by-sa/2.0>, via Wikimedia Commons: https://commons.wikimedia.org/wiki/File:Gutenberg_Bible,_Lenox_Copy,_New_York_Public_Library,_2009._Pic_01.jpg

[38] https://pixabay.com/illustrations/sunset-island-sea-silhouette-girl-485016/

[39] HOWI – Horsch, Willy, CC BY-SA 4.0 <https://creativecommons.org/licenses/by-sa/4.0>, via Wikimedia Commons: https://commons.wikimedia.org/wiki/File:K%C3%B6ln-Tora-und-Innenansicht-Synagoge-Glockengasse-040.JPG

[40] John Snyder, CC BY-SA 3.0 <https://creativecommons.org/licenses/by-sa/3.0>, via Wikimedia Commons https://commons.wikimedia.org/wiki/File:The_Book_of_Genesis.jpg

[41] https://commons.wikimedia.org/wiki/File:Edward_Hicks,_American_-_Noah%27s_Ark_-_Google_Art_Project.jpg

[42] *Distant Shores Media/Sweet Publishing, CC BY-SA 3.0* <*https://creativecommons.org/licenses/by-sa/3.0*>, *via Wikimedia Commons* https://commons.wikimedia.org/wiki/File:Book_of_Exodus_Chapter_15-7_%28Bible_Illustrations_by_Sweet_Media%29.jpg

[43] *Distant Shores Media/Sweet Publishing, CC BY-SA 3.0* <*https://creativecommons.org/licenses/by-sa/3.0*>, *via Wikimedia Commons* https://commons.wikimedia.org/wiki/File:Book_of_Deuteronomy_Chapter_32-4_%28Bible_Illustrations_by_Sweet_Media%29.jpg

[44] *https://pixabay.com/illustrations/grateful-thankful-appreciation-1988951/*

[45] *https://www.pexels.com/photo/close-up-of-book-in-jewish-15126093/*

[46] *Henk Monster, CC BY 3.0* <*https://creativecommons.org/licenses/by/3.0*>, *via Wikimedia Commons* https://commons.wikimedia.org/wiki/File:King_David_playing_at_his_harp_in_the_St_Bavochurch_Haarlem_-_panoramio.jpg

[47] *https://www.pexels.com/photo/text-on-a-white-paper-11506033/*

[48] *https://www.pexels.com/photo/writing-typography-blur-business-14274670/*

[49] *See page for author, CC BY 4.0* <*https://creativecommons.org/licenses/by/4.0*>, *via Wikimedia Commons* https://commons.wikimedia.org/wiki/File:Death,_symbolism;_three_skeletons_with_roundel_of_corpses,_Wellcome_L0000680.jpg

[50] *https://pixabay.com/illustrations/bible-prophecy-cross-christianity-2062081/*

[51] *Missional Volunteer, CC BY-SA 2.0* <*https://creativecommons.org/licenses/by-sa/2.0*>, *via Wikimedia Commons* https://commons.wikimedia.org/wiki/File:Isaiah_%281%29.jpg

[52] *Giorgio Ghisi, CC0, via Wikimedia Commons* https://commons.wikimedia.org/wiki/File:The_Prophet_Jeremiah,_from_the_series_of_Prophets_and_Sibyls_in_the_Sistine_Chapel_MET_DP821566.jpg

[53] *Giorgio Ghisi, CC0, via Wikimedia Commons* https://commons.wikimedia.org/wiki/File:The_Prophet_Ezekiel;_from_the_series_of_Prophets_and_Sibyls_in_the_Sistine_Chapel_MET_DP821561.jpg

[54] *Ted, Attribution-ShareAlike 2.0 Generic, CC BY-SA 2.0 DEED* <*https://creativecommons.org/licenses/by-sa/2.0/* > https://www.flickr.com/photos/frted/5692055059

[55] *Hans Bernhard (Schnobby), CC BY-SA 3.0* <*https://creativecommons.org/licenses/by-sa/3.0*>, *via Wikimedia Commons* https://commons.wikimedia.org/wiki/File:Prophet_Hosea_in_Augsburg_Cathedral.jpg

[56] *Giorgio Ghisi, CC0, via Wikimedia Commons* https://commons.wikimedia.org/wiki/File:The_Prophet_Joel;_from_the_series_of_Prophets_and_Sibyls_in_the_Sistine_Chapel_MET_DP821553.jpg

[57] *Ted, Attribution-ShareAlike 2.0 Generic CC BY-SA 2.0 DEED* <*https://creativecommons.org/licenses/by-sa/2.0/*> https://www.flickr.com/photos/frted/6995565615

[58] Sailko, CC BY 3.0 <https://creativecommons.org/licenses/by/3.0>, via Wikimedia Commons https://commons.wikimedia.org/wiki/File:Melozzo_da_forl%C3%AC,_angeli_coi_simboli_della_pa ssione_e_profeti,_1477_ca.,_profeta_abdia_01.jpg

[59] PravoslavnyChristianin, CC0, через Викисклад https://commons.wikimedia.org/wiki/File:Prophet_Nahum.webp?uselang=ru

[60] Ted, Attribution-ShareAlike 2.0 Generic CC BY-SA 2.0 DEED <https://creativecommons.org/licenses/by-sa/2.0/> https://www.flickr.com/photos/frted/5692625836

[61] George E. Koronaios, CC BY-SA 4.0 <https://creativecommons.org/licenses/by-sa/4.0>, via Wikimedia Commons https://commons.wikimedia.org/wiki/File:Mural_depicting_the_ Prophet_Zephaniah_%28Sophonias%29_at_the_Cathedral_of_Athens_on_June_4,_2022.jpg

[62] Jojojoe, CC BY-SA 3.0 <https://creativecommons.org/licenses/by-sa/3.0>, via Wikimedia Commons https://commons.wikimedia.org/wiki/File:Zechariah_Hajdudorog.JPG

[63] See page for author, CC BY 4.0 <https://creativecommons.org/licenses/by/4.0>, via Wikimedia Commons https://commons.wikimedia.org/wiki/File:The_Four_Gospels,_1495,_Gospel _of_St_John_4;_43-46,_s_Wellcome_L0031113.jpg

[64] User:Murphnspud101, CC BY-SA 3.0 <https://creativecommons.org/licenses/by-sa/3.0>, via Wikimedia Commons https://commons.wikimedia.org/wiki/File:Jesus_Christ_2014-05-19_10- 06.jpg

[65] Farragutful, CC BY-SA 4.0 <https://creativecommons.org/licenses/by-sa/4.0>, via Wikimedia Commons https://commons.wikimedia.org/wiki/File:Saint_Andrew_-_Roanoke_interior_01.jpg

[66] Ted, Attribution-ShareAlike 2.0 Generic CC BY-SA 2.0 DEED <https://creativecommons.org/licenses/by-sa/2.0/> https://www.flickr.com/photos/frted/5692052863

[67] https://www.pexels.com/photo/close-up-shot-of-a-person-reading-a-book-with-rosary-5206844/

[68] FlippyFlink, CC BY-SA 4.0 <https://creativecommons.org/licenses/by-sa/4.0>, via Wikimedia Commons: https://commons.wikimedia.org/wiki/File:King_James_Bible-New_Testament.jpg

[69] https://pixabay.com/vectors/end-hourglass-the-end-mysterious-4109186/

[70] https://www.pexels.com/photo/scriptures-from-a-bible-5247486/

[71] https://pixabay.com/vectors/business-idea-style-concept-goals-1753098/

Made in United States
Troutdale, OR
02/08/2025

28779124R00149